My Life in My Hands

ALISON LAPPER

with GUY FELDMAN

POCKET
BOOKS

LONDON • SYDNEY • NEW YORK • TORONTO

First published in Great Britain by Simon & Schuster UK Ltd, 2005
This edition published by Pocket Books, 2006
An imprint of Simon & Schuster UK Ltd
A CBS COMPANY

1 3 5 7 9 10 8 6 4 2

Simon & Schuster UK Ltd
Africa House
64–78 Kingsway
London WC2B 6AH

www.simonsays.co.uk

Simon & Schuster Australia
Sydney

A CIP catalogue record for this book is available from the British Library.

ISBN 1-4165-1101-6
EAN 9781416511014

Printed and bound in Great Britain by
Cox & Wyman Ltd, Reading, Berks

For Parys

Thanks to Mark Dawkins
who inspired me to write this book

Contents

	Prologue	1
1	It's a Girl, Mrs Lapper	11
2	Home Sweet Home	19
3	Norfolk Days	38
4	Mummy Dearest	54
5	Lower Dorm	72
6	Upper Dorm	92
7	Boyfriends	121
8	Banstead	135
9	Living in London	160
10	Wedding Bells	168
11	Alison Lapper, Artist	178
12	My First House and a Surprise	189
13	Parys	206
14	Meeting Michael	216
15	The Statue in Trafalgar Square	234

Prologue

A tall policeman in a yellow reflective jacket leaned down at the driver's window of the limo and said: 'Can I see your invitation, please?' I waited in the back with my friends as he checked the papers. We were parked outside the gates of Buckingham Palace in a long queue of luxury cars – Bentleys, Rolls-Royces, a few limousines like the one I had hired for the day – and the occasional family car looking slightly out of place. It was a bright sunny day in May 2003 and several people who also had invitations for the Palace were chatting on the pavement. I could see uniformed admirals and generals, men in morning suits, and ladies wearing dresses like those seen at Royal Ascot. There were also many people from other countries wearing their national costumes. Everyone looked very smart and elegant and I had a momentary pang of anxiety. My dress had been bought from a second-hand shop in Arundel which sold designer clothes. It was made from white knitted silk with red accessories and had been specially taken in and adjusted for my shape. It had looked very fine in the shop when I bought it but now I wondered if it would match up to the quality of the clothes I could see outside. I mentioned my fears to my friends but they all said my dress was beautiful and that I looked very good wearing it.

A few months earlier I had received a letter from the Palace informing me that I'd been awarded the MBE for services to the arts. I was shocked because it came completely out of the blue. My first thought was that it was someone's idea of a practical joke. How could it possibly be for me? I rang my friend Peter Hull, who had received an MBE himself ten years earlier. I told him I'd received a prank letter in the post and what should I do about it. After I'd read it out to him, he said: 'Don't worry, Alison, that letter is from the Palace. It's real.' I put the phone down and felt reassured though I was still in a daze. I had no idea who had nominated me or why but I felt grateful to whoever it was. I was asked in the letter if I would accept the medal and whether I would like to receive it from the Queen at Buckingham Palace on 8 May. There was no doubt that I would go. I love special occasions of any kind and to my mind there was very little that was more special than going to Buckingham Palace and receiving an award from the Queen herself. I was also prohibited from telling anyone about it until it was announced in the New Year's Honours List. That last proviso was torture for me because I was dying to tell everyone I knew.

The letter explained that I could bring three guests and they were now alongside me in the long white limo. Sue and Jane were close friends and the third was my boyfriend, Michael. There was also a cameraman with us from Danish television but he had been filming me on and off for five years so I didn't feel inhibited by his presence.

That morning the five of us had driven the sixty miles from my home in Shoreham. It was a long journey, more than three hours, but we were all in extremely high spirits. The limousine had bottles of champagne on ice for us but we didn't want to drink it until after the ceremony. The thought of turning up at the Palace rather tipsy and toppling over as I walked the red carpet to receive my honour from the Queen stopped me from indulging, although I was very tempted. In the meantime we enjoyed the scenery and the luxurious feeling of being chauffeur-driven.

The limo had darkened windows so we could see what was happening in the outside world but it couldn't see us. As we came up through Croydon, people stared at the car as if wondering which famous celebrity might be inside. I wonder what their reaction would have been if I had wound down the window and said hello. I think they would have had a shock because not only would they probably not have recognized me but they would have seen that I had no arms, that I was disabled. Even in the twenty-first century people are generally uncomfortable when they see a disabled person. I'm sure seeing me seated in the back of a stretch limo wearing a long silk dress would have been doubly confusing and most likely disappointing. With a few notable exceptions – Stephen

Hawking, Tanni Grey-Thompson and Heather Mills – disabled people are not celebrities.

As we waited, the cameraman decided that this would be a good opportunity to get some exterior footage and got out to take pictures of Buckingham Palace with our limo in the foreground. He had barely adjusted his tripod and started filming when the queue of cars began to move. We all laughed as he came scuttling back with his equipment under his arm.

We had been rehearsing little disaster scenarios, probably because we were all nervous. My dress would split. The invitation would be spotted as a forgery. They were very sorry, there had been a mistake and it was another Alison Lapper who was going to get the MBE for services to the arts. But all that nervous talk was forgotten as we swept through the palace gates and into the inner quadrangle.

It was the first time I had ever been inside the gates of Buckingham Palace. I had never really given much thought to the royal family and what they did. As far as I was concerned they inhabited a world as far removed from mine as I could possibly imagine. They had always seemed to me to be something from a bygone age which still existed but which didn't have much to do, for good or ill, with ordinary people like myself. But as I walked along under the tall pillars of the colonnade and into the Palace itself, some of the power of the monarchy and its history began to make themselves felt. The huge paintings on the walls and the massively high ceilings which towered above me accentuated the gravity and importance of the occasion. And when I looked at the printed programme which listed all the people who were receiving awards that day I saw that the great majority were being acknowledged for decades of unstinting public service. I won't say that I felt like a fraud but it was humbling. I began to get a sense of the honour it was for me to be there.

At a certain point they divided us into groups alphabetically and we were led into the picture gallery where Rembrandts and Canalettos hung on the walls. The master of ceremonies explained what would happen and how we were to behave in front of the Queen. Our first words to her should be 'Your Majesty' and after that we should address her as 'ma'am'. We should never turn our back on her at any time and when she had finished talking to us she would signal with a handshake or, as in my case, a tap on the shoulder. We should then retreat backwards until we were no longer in her presence.

I was assigned a young man called Ian, who was one of the Queen's pages. He assisted me in the picture gallery and stayed with me as we walked through to the ballroom where the Queen was officiating. I asked him how long it would be before it was my turn and he said about forty minutes. I explained that I couldn't stand for that long so he arranged for me to have a seat at the front where I could watch proceedings while he took my place in the queue. He asked if I'd like him to walk out with me when it was my turn to meet the Queen and I said yes because I'd feel awkward if I fell over as someone would have to pick me up. I was very grateful for Ian's presence because by then I was extremely nervous. It was a very grand occasion and in addition there were 400 other people in the room all watching me, which added to the pressure.

Finally my name was called and Ian walked forwards with me. When I arrived at the dais I said 'Your Majesty' and bowed as I had been instructed. The Queen said she was going to come down and stepped off the podium to bring herself to my level. I told her it was a good job she did or she would have had to bend down a long way to get to me. The Queen laughed and asked me about my art and about my son, Parys, and about what my next project was going to be. I was impressed by her. She had the ability to talk to anyone about anything and it didn't matter what field of endeavour they came from. Of course, I realize she has had years of practice.

She talked with me for what seemed like a long time but was probably only thirty seconds. She placed my MBE medal on the little hook that had been fixed on to me in the picture gallery and said congratulations. Then I received my little tap on the shoulder. Ian, who had been waiting a few steps back, came forward and we both retreated from the royal presence together. When we got to the back of the room he said: 'See, you didn't fall over. In fact, you did very well up there.'

There were another forty or so people to receive decorations so I sat at the back with Ian and waited till the end. When they played 'God Save the Queen' I felt moved by the music for the first and probably only time.

As I emerged once again into the bright sunshine of the quadrangle I felt like I was walking on air. The BBC's *Child of Our Time* crew were waiting to do an interview with me and the Danish TV cameraman, as always, was filming my every move. The BBC asked me how I had felt when I received my MBE from the Queen but they also had more probing questions and I became quite tearful when they asked me why I hadn't brought Parys with me to the Palace. I would dearly have loved to but I knew that the event was too long for him. He would have been bored and temperamental. So he didn't come.

I then completed an interview for Danish television and after that had my photograph taken by one of the several official photographers in the quad. A few feet from me Edward Fox, the actor, and his family were having their photograph taken, too. I think it's fair to say that I was basking in the sunshine of the occasion and had no desire to move. Ian strolled over to our group and we shared a joke or two. He explained to me the differences between a page and a footman, the Palace hierarchy and various aspects of life below stairs. I was riveted by what he had to say because up to that day I had known nothing whatsoever about Palace life. It was a very heady atmosphere. I was surrounded by the great, the good and the famous and felt very much part of their crowd. My seventeen childhood years at the institution for the disabled seemed a long time ago.

We lingered in the Palace quadrangle till we could linger no more. It was three o'clock by the time we found ourselves driving up Pall Mall. The first bottle of champagne was opened and everyone toasted the occasion. As we drained our glasses the driver turned into the little cul-de-sac off the Strand where the Savoy hotel is situated. I had booked a table for lunch to be sure that this was a day to remember. The service was superb. It seemed as if I only had to think of something that I wanted and a waiter would be at my side.

The food was beautiful to look at and tasted equally good. And two of the pages I had made friends with earlier came over from another table and squatted beside me to have a chat. They had both cruised with Prince Philip on the royal yacht *Britannia* and had interesting tales to tell. We were all still high from the excitement of the ceremony and I was loving every minute.

By the time we got ourselves back into the limo for our journey to Shoreham it was getting dark. We opened another bottle of champagne and reviewed various moments from the day. As we drove south through the outskirts of London the conversation faltered and everyone became quiet for a while. I was thinking about the medal I still had pinned on to my dress and trying to put the day's events into some sort of perspective. On one level I acknowledged the honour as personal to me. But I also thought of it as belonging in a way to disabled people everywhere. We are a disadvantaged group in society who most people find difficult to relate to. We are an awkward nuisance for most people and they usually deal with us by not dealing with us. There is a phrase which says children should be seen and not heard. I think there is a similar implicit phrase which says disabled people should not be seen and not heard. And many disabled people live their lives conforming to that idea. They give in to the pressures; the staring, the impatient looks and disgusted faces.

I have felt the same pressures myself but for some reason I cannot explain I have always refused to let those pressures limit the way in which I have wanted to live my life. I have been driven by the idea that my life can be as full as anyone else's, no matter what other people think. In fact, it has been precisely those times when people told me that I couldn't do something that I became the most determined to prove them wrong. The only difference for me is that I have always known that I would have to work harder than able-bodied people to achieve what I wanted. And one of the biggest obstacles to my progress has been their prejudice and limited view of what I could achieve.

I accept that it's easy for me to complain that disabled people are discriminated against and not properly catered for by our infrastructure. Changes are being made and things *are* slowly getting better, but the level of access provided for disabled people in the United Kingdom is often below European standards and institutional discrimination is as well established as ever. For example, there are very few disabled doctors in the United Kingdom. Unless people with impairments like me are willing to share what it's like to live our lives, the rest of the population will never be able to appreciate the difficulties we face. How can I accuse people of having no understanding of disability and then refuse to tell them anything about my personal life. It was on that day at the Palace that I came to the conclusion that telling my life's story was the best way for me to make the issues I care about understood.

1

It's a Girl, Mrs Lapper

*I*t was 8 April 1965, the day after I was born. My mother lay
alone in a small room at the hospital in Burton-upon-Trent.
She had been sedated by the hospital staff and couldn't think
very clearly. All she knew was that she'd been brought in to
have her baby in hospital because it had been in breech position. It had all been very rushed and sudden. Now she lay
there feeling limp, her mind foggy with the tranquillizers. She
couldn't remember anything about the birth – nothing from
the moment that they administered the anaesthetic. But she
did remember that she had come into hospital to have a baby.
Where was the baby now? Why hadn't they brought it in for

her to see? There was nobody in the room to ask and after a while she drifted back into sleep.

My mother came from a working-class family who lived in Birmingham. She had married Gordon Lapper, and they had a daughter, Vanessa, who was eight years old when I was born. The marriage hadn't worked out. It seems that Gordon didn't like children and since Vanessa was the apple of my mother's eye she had decided to leave him and go back to live with her parents. I later asked my mother how I had come to be conceived and she told me that she and Gordon had been trying to make a go of the marriage again, for Vanessa's sake. She soon realized that it wasn't going to work but in the meantime had become pregnant with me. That is the story she told me. I'm not sure if they were divorced when she got pregnant. Nevertheless, there was some stigma attached to the pregnancy and my mother decided to avoid local gossip and any unpleasant remarks by spending the last few months at her best friend Sylvia's house in Tamworth.

The pregnancy went well, with no difficulties or complications. Vanessa was being looked after by my grandparents in their home and my mother, Veronica, was enjoying her stay with her best friend. The final three weeks seemed to crawl by but finally the long-awaited day arrived. My mother went into labour and Sylvia called the midwife who came round to the flat and examined her. The waters had broken and regular contractions had set in but the midwife also discovered that the baby was breech. That's all she told my mother at the time but I suspect she knew there were other complications. In those days, doctors and nurses were much less open and informative than they are now. The midwife explained to my mother that it was no longer safe to have the baby at home and she sent for an ambulance to take her into the local maternity unit at the hospital in Burton-upon-Trent, which attended to women who had difficulty giving birth.

She could hear the sounds of hospital life outside her door and once or twice a nurse came in to check on her, but they never said anything apart from asking her to take another tranquillizer. Later in the day a cleaner came in the room to tidy up and mop the floor. She looked up at my mother lying in her hospital bed and noticed that she was awake. She was the chatty sort of woman you meet amongst hospital ancillary staff.

'Can you hear all that screaming down the corridor? That's a baby that's just been born. She's in a terrible state. She's got no arms or legs and there's a big red mark all across her face. It's a horrible looking thing. The nurses say she'll die in a day or two, or else be a cabbage for the rest of her life. It's a proper little monster, I can tell you. And I heard one of the nurses talking about it. There's a bit of a panic going on. They don't know what to do. Neither do the doctors. I expect they're waiting for it to die.'

Of course, the baby was me but my mother didn't know that. She felt sorry for that distressed baby in the maternity unit. She wondered where its mother was and how she was going to cope with all that screaming. The cleaner finished her mopping and left the room, closing the door quietly behind her. My mother lay there in a daze, hearing the distant but continual screams and vaguely wondering where her own baby was.

The next day one of the nurses came in looking worried and uncomfortable. It was her duty to deliver the first piece of official information. I wonder how they chose her, the person who was going to be the unlucky bearer of bad tidings. She was professional and direct. She told my mother that she'd had a baby that was seriously deformed and probably wouldn't live more than a few days. And, in any case, if it did manage to survive it would almost certainly be a cabbage. I don't know if she actually used the word 'cabbage' but that's what my mother remembers. The nurse added that it would probably be best if she didn't see her baby just yet.

My mother listened blank-faced. It was very hard for her to take in. There was the horror and mystery of the announcement. How deformed? She thought it must be pretty bad if I was only going to last a few days. Then came the shock when she realized why she hadn't been allowed to see her baby. And finally there was the shame and the guilt and the 'what would the neighbours think' and the 'why me?' and a hundred other vicious thoughts all attacking at once. How was she going to cope with it all? There was nobody from the hospital to counsel her, sympathize, hold her hand or even sit by her bedside for a while. I imagine the hospital staff, from doctors to cleaners, were horrified at how impaired I was. My mother must have been disappointed that none of them spent time comforting her.

At that point my mother sank back into her pillows and

drifted bit by bit into a deep depression. She only had one thought: to get out of the hospital and return home. That afternoon, when her head had cleared a little, she tried to leave the hospital wearing just her nightclothes. She managed to get halfway down the corridor but was spotted by one of the nurses who intercepted her and immediately shouted for help. With the alarm ringing two nursing auxiliaries raced up from the maternity ward and the three of them bundled her back into bed. The sister in charge was called in. Without saying a word she put all my mother's clothes in a bag and took the bag away, locking the door behind her.

A few hours later my mother heard a key in the lock. The door opened and one of the hospital administrators entered the room. His face was grim and unsmiling as he gave her a stern lecture about her legal position and responsibilities. He finished by saying that if she tried to leave the hospital again they'd take her to the local police station and have her arrested. She was quite certain he meant every word he said.

Another two days went by during which my mother was kept sedated. She was visited by all the family but nobody seemed to know what was happening with her baby. I'm sure the hospital authorities were having difficulty deciding what to do. I wonder whether they were waiting to see whether I would die, which would have solved the problem of having to sort things out. But I didn't die.

On Good Friday another nurse unlocked the door to my mother's room and came and stood with her clipboard by my mother's bedside.

'Mrs Lapper, we really don't think your baby is going to

last very much longer, maybe just a day or two, so we must give her a name today – for the birth certificate. Do you have a name?'

'Alison,' she replied.

I was given no middle names. I was just Alison Lapper, end of story. All through the pregnancy my mother had intended to call me Francesca but when asked for a name it was Alison that popped out. She has no idea why.

My mother was released from hospital that same day and her parents took her back to their home. She was virtually catatonic and spent day after day sitting in a chair in their front room without uttering a word. One morning her father brought her a bunch of flowers to cheer her up. He put them in a vase next to her chair and sat down beside her.

'If only you'd just talk to us, love. Just say something,' he said.

But she didn't respond. Her mother helped to look after her, too, but she took a much harder line than her father. It was probably her old-fashioned attitude of 'pull yourself together and get on with your life'. What was done was done and there was no point in moping about it. My mother admits she has the same streak of hardness herself.

About a week later she was considered well enough to be taken to her regular GP for a checkup. After she had been physically examined – she was still very sore because she had been badly stitched at the hospital – she plucked up enough courage to ask the doctor about me. His response was very direct and to the point. He told my mother it would be best if I were looked after by the state and that she should put me out of her mind. He said the same thing to my grandparents and from then on I was rarely mentioned by the family. In due course, my mother returned to her work as a machinist at the Lucas car components factory and was able to erase me entirely from her mind. I was no longer a factor in her life.

I used to get extremely upset and angry about it in later years, but I never blamed her. I can see why she reacted to me in the way she did, especially considering the way the hospital dealt with her. Imagine being told that your child is deformed, probably brain-damaged and that you'd better christen her quickly before she dies. I am pretty certain that in those days giving birth to a baby with missing limbs was considered a horror – a terrible and shameful thing. Some people would have thought of it as a punishment from God, and that is still a popular view in some quarters. Others, perhaps the nurses and doctors, would have thought it was one of nature's abominations, a catastrophe so extreme that no medical procedure could put it right. It would have been very hard for anyone at all to have any kind of positive attitude about my arrival in the world.

So there I was. Alison Lapper, aged one week. With no arms. And my legs had no knees, just the thigh bone ending in my feet, which weren't quite right either. I looked like a thalidomide child but my actual condition was phocomelia. The *On-Line Medical Dictionary* says: 'A congenital malformation (birth defect) in which the hands and feet are attached to abbreviated arms and legs. The word phocomelia combines phoco- (seal) and melia (limb) to designate a limb like a seal's flipper.' Nobody knew what caused it, but since I looked very similar to the earlier thalidomide cases most people assumed that's what I was. I was considered to be severely disabled. I hate that phrase with a passion, but that was the label that was attached to me for the next nineteen years.

2

Home Sweet Home

*I*t was decided by the authorities that it would be best for all concerned if I was taken into care. The place they had chosen for me in the south of England suddenly developed a chickenpox epidemic and that was considered unsafe for a one-week-old baby. So I was put in a private old people's nursing home and then, sometime before I was seven weeks old, I was shipped to the children's home where I remained for the whole of my childhood.

In 1965 it was thought that disabled children shouldn't live at home with their parents. It was better to put them away somewhere where they could be properly taken care of and there was little help to keep children at home. In truth, it was

_____

the parents who needed the help more than we did or, at least, just as much. And, of course, they didn't get any. No counselling, just silence.

My new home was considered to be one of the best places for a child with a physical disability. It catered for mental disability, too. I don't know why they so often put the mentally disabled and physically disabled children together in the same institutions. Perhaps they found it difficult to distinguish between the two. I know the nurses were always surprised to find me talking and drawing and showing all the signs of normal childhood intelligence.

So there we were, about 250 children with a variety of impairments: thalidomides, spina bifidas, cerebral palsies, limb-deficients, mentally deficients and many other types of impairment, all lumped together on one big residential site. The staff called us 'the strange little creatures' and did their best to cope with us in what I think was essentially an experimental situation. Nurse Shepherd, a compassionate, caring woman who was one of the few adults I trusted there, said to me once: 'We didn't know what to do with you. You couldn't sit up, you couldn't stand . . . you . . . you couldn't do anything.'

The staff put a lot of their energies into dealing with our basic needs – feeding us, housing us, keeping us clean – but in a very regimented and Victorian way. Our buildings were a large self-contained group of institutional facilities and they all seemed huge to us. One building, a massive exception to the general style on the site, was built like a Benedictine monastery, with long cloisters and high pale stone walls. I used to wonder why they chose to have a building like that. Were we supposed to grow up and become monks and nuns?

Looking back I can see that the home, like so many institutions of that type, had certain undercurrents. People found it hard to come to terms with us. We kids with our missing limbs and twisted bodies just looked too different, too strange compared to the norm. And some of them thought our condition must be due to some kind of punishment from God. So there was an underlying sense of us having been bad somehow and that we needed to be good, good to the point of even being holy. Maybe the monastic look of that building was designed to help us along that road. If it was, I can tell you it didn't have that effect on me.

The nurses were very old-fashioned and strict and wore a blue uniform covered with a long, flowing navy-blue cape fastened at the front with wide, red crossed bands. They wore a starched hat like a little square pillbox and a white apron which was pinned on to the blue uniform beneath. And I remember that their stiff uniforms rustled as they wheeled us babies and toddlers around in huge sprung Victorian prams, often four to a pram.

We progressed from building to building according to our age. As a very young baby I was in the baby section and I don't remember anything about it. Then at about six months I moved into another unit, where I stayed until I was eighteen months old. I don't remember anything about that time either, except the smell, but that must have been when I first got to know Nurse Shepherd because she always worked there. Then I was moved to Alban Block One [not its real name] where I stayed until I was three. And next stop was Alban Block Two [not its real name]. The blocks were long, rectangular red-brick buildings with metal French doors along their length. The interior walls were painted white or pale green and the floors were made of bare concrete with occasional patches of lino. Every other unit had an odour of disinfectant and stale cabbage but the infant section smelled totally different. It had a sweet baby smell which it never lost in all the seventeen years I was there. Whenever I went there in later years the smell enveloped me in a feeling of warmth and security.

But although it smelled sweet and warm the nurses there were very strict with the babies. Some years after I had left, I was making one of my return visits to see Nurse Shepherd and on my way I thought I would take a look at the babies in their cots. They were all sleeping peacefully. Then one of the babies began to cry. I looked around not knowing what to do but a nursing auxiliary came in to see what was the matter. She was about to take it out of its cot to comfort it when the nurse in charge came bustling through the nursery door. She barked: 'Put that baby down! There is no need to pick up these babies. They don't need hugs!' She said it as if giving a baby a hug or picking one up if it was crying was tantamount to giving it some kind of poisonous drug. It was a strange reversal of thinking, as if the baby might somehow be irretrievably damaged by a hug. That was the attitude that prevailed there, although not all the staff behaved in that way.

By the age of one or two I think we all somehow knew

we had been abandoned and, in varying degrees, we were traumatized by the fact. The idea of having been abandoned ran very deep in me and the other children, and it had huge emotional power. We had all heard about what had happened to one of the children who had been taken there by his parents when he was two years old. They brought him down to the home and explained when they left him behind that they would be back again in a few weeks and that it wouldn't be long. Naturally the little boy missed them desperately and couldn't wait for his parents to come and see him again. And they did come down as they had promised him, for one weekend and then another. But at the end of the second visit, after they had kissed their son, given him a little hug and said goodbye to him, they drove out of the gates and simply never came back. His deformity had just been too much for them to cope with. The authorities couldn't find any trace of them and he never saw them again. Most of us felt a little or a lot like him. Even though some of the children had parents who visited them from time to time they weren't necessarily very happy occasions. One particular mother always burst into tears every time she came to visit her daughter.

In any case, even when any of us received a visit from parents or relatives we knew that the visit would end in a couple of days and then we would be left behind once again. And none of us could really understand why. I'm sure some parents told their children how it was the *best* thing for them to be there, where they would get all the *best* help in the world from the *best* professionals in the world who were wise and

23

experienced and knew much better than their mum and dad what was *best* for them.

The basic fact for us was that we didn't live cosily at home with our mums and dads. And we came to understand very well that we lived in this other place that wasn't at all homely and which didn't have things like mums and dads. Instead we had things called Sister Jones and Matron Smith and Nurse Shepherd – the staff.

The nursing staff had been taught that it was not advisable to get close to the children, so they were not very affectionate or loving. I don't blame them for that because it was the official policy. It was thought to be best for all concerned if any actions which might lead to any kind of emotional attachment were avoided. But, of course, we tiny little children were desperate for some love from an adult. Studies have shown that this is natural and necessary but the authorities didn't see it that way.

I developed a bond with Nurse Shepherd, who was lovely and old-fashioned. I don't know exactly how long it took but over time it dawned on me that Nurse Shepherd really cared about my welfare and, in so far as the rules of nursing there allowed, showed me as much affection and attention as was possible for her. She was also very starchy, like many of the nurses, and totally committed to fulfilling her nursing duties in a thoroughly professional manner. For her, nursing was a vocation, not just a job. But at the same time she was warm-hearted and cheerful. I could tell that she did her best to look after me and to look out for me. She also treated me as if I was a worthwhile sensible human being, even when I was naughty or wayward. The connection we established continued during my time there and remains as strong as ever today. Looking back I wonder what would have happened to me if I hadn't had her support and love in those very early years.

Since the staff were unwilling or not allowed to get close to us, we children, naturally enough, looked to each other for friendship. At an early age I became very close to a boy called Phil (not his real name). He was my first real friend and nurses who knew us told me later that we were inseparable. I can only remember that he was the most important person in my life at the time.

In the early years, before I started going to the school, my life had two aspects. First, there was the domestic side of things: eating, sleeping, washing and socializing. And then there was the medical side where we would be examined, looked at, photographed and appraised by a continual visitation of various groups of doctors. A nurse would come to the dorm, consult the list on her clipboard, and call out the names. The chosen group would toddle outside where a kind of handcart was waiting. It was a bit like a small cattle truck with very high sides and no roof. It was impossible to see anything once you were in and the tailgate was pulled up. Of course, there were no seat belts or safety devices and we just rolled from side to side in a jumble of bodies as the porters wheeled us over to the medical wing for physiotherapy.

Once there, a nurse would help me up on to an examining table, where I would lie naked or sometimes with just my knickers on while a group of ten to fifteen older medical professionals would make a circle around me. They would then poke this part or pull that part or rotate another part, all the while conversing in that detached medic-speak which is impossible to understand if you are not a doctor yourself. And sometimes they took photographs. They rarely addressed me and I could tell that I was just an object of curiosity for them, nothing more. And even at the age of four, something made me feel vulnerable and uncomfortable in that situation. No doubt they were gazing at me with purely detached and scientific interest but it still didn't seem quite right. Of course, there was no question of anyone asking our permission. We somehow weren't quite human enough to be asked if we were happy to be sprawled naked on the table for examination by the medical profession.

The staff on the medical side were constantly engaged in trying to fix us up, to make us work better or look better. And fixing us up, for the doctors, mostly meant operating on us. One of my earliest memories was of Phil, aged two and a half, who had just come back from an operation. The sister in charge knew that he and I were friendly with each other and when I kept asking her where Phil was she eventually gave in and allowed me to go and see him in the recovery room.

He was lying very still in a metal cot with high sides. His arm was suspended to keep it raised and blood was slowly seeping out through the white bandage which they had put on after the operation. He was in pain and crying. I went in to see him every day after that and he was always crying. He looked totally helpless, which he was. And I remember standing by his bed and feeling totally helpless myself. I wanted to do something, to help him somehow but there was absolutely nothing I could do to take away his pain and make him feel better. I suppose you could say these were the two major threads of my life at the home: feeling helpless and feeling pain.

Phil's hand eventually healed and we continued our friendship when he returned to the dorm. But at around the age of three, Phil disappeared from my life and I never saw him again. One day he was there and the next day his bed was empty and nobody knew anything about it. The nurses were tight-lipped and refused to answer any of my questions. I think they genuinely thought that I didn't need to know and that it was none of my business.

Soon after Phil had gone I made friends with two other children, Peter Hull and Tara Flood. Peter had no legs, just his upper torso and two pointy stumps for arms. He was steadfast and loyal, what I would call a good all-rounder. And as an adult he later won gold and silver medals for swimming at the Paralympics as well as receiving an MBE from the Queen. Tara had short truncated legs and arm stumps that didn't extend as far as her elbows would have been. She was the 'bright one', destined for university and the glittering prize of a top-flight career. We were all very different in our fundamental characters but still became a close-knit trio of adventurers and mischief-makers. The three of us must have been quite a handful for the staff. They were always trying to separate us, but the harder they tried the more we clung together.

One winter we were playing in our playroom in Alban

Block when Peter and I heard Tara say: 'Hey look!' We both looked out of the window to where she was pointing and saw clusters of big white snowflakes slowly drifting down from the sky and settling on the ground. We had never seen snow before and, like all children, we were completely captivated by the way it fell and how it gradually created a thick white carpet on the ground outside. We stopped playing, and talking, and watched the falling snow for a long time until it had created a layer several inches thick. It seemed magical and wonderful to us.

We kept on talking about it during lunch and kept glancing out of the dining-room windows to make sure it was still there. The next morning before we got dressed, we decided it would be a good idea to explore the magical qualities of snow by going out and playing in it, and even better, we decided to go naked. We were convinced that running about in the freshly fallen snow with no clothes on would be the best fun of all. And it *was* good fun. We scooted snow on to each other with whatever limbs or partial limbs that we had. And we raced round playing tag, rolling down the sloping banks and shoving each other into the deeper drifts. We had a sense that we were being naughty, too, but that added to the thrill. The fun couldn't last, of course. We were spotted rolling around outside, squealing and laughing, and one of the sisters came out to see what was going on.

'What on earth do you think you are doing!'

'Playing in the snow, Sister.'

'I can see that. But you haven't got any clothes on!'

'No, we haven't, Sister.'

'And why haven't you got any clothes on?'

'Don't know, Sister.'

We may have giggled a little at first but we could tell we were all in big trouble and quickly lost our cheekiness and laughter.

Other staff emerged from the building and we were dragged off inside and shouted at by the senior sister. I'm not sure which offence they considered more serious: rolling about in the snow or being naked. They assumed that it was Peter who was the ringleader in this escapade and that he must have been the one who had persuaded us poor innocent girls to get our kits off. Presumably they thought he needed to satisfy his terrible desire to look at naked 3-year-old girls in the snow, which, as we all know, is every 3-year-old boy's fantasy. If anything it was Tara and myself who had to persuade Peter to go outside for a little snow-romping. He was the shyest of us three. But that possibility didn't occur to the nurse. Girls were, after all, sugar and spice and all things nice; well, compared to boys anyway.

The episode in the snow led to a further attempt to separate us. Many of the staff thought our close friendship was unhealthy and that we were too disruptive when we got together in our gang of three. They decided to deal with the situation by putting me into a girls-only unit. I hated it. I hardly ever saw my friends and it had a play area which I didn't like. The dormitory was on the upper floor of the building and the only area they provided for us to play in was a wide, round concrete balcony which was hard and cold, winter and summer. It was impossible to see through the concrete wall of the balcony so I felt completely isolated and enclosed when I played there. The whole point was to give us an outside play area but the balcony felt like I was still indoors. I much preferred the grass outside the ground floor dormitory I had been used to.

I was also feeling hard done by. I thought that I had been unjustly picked out and was being labelled as some kind of troublemaker. It was often assumed, even if it was the tiniest of incidents, that anything untoward that happened was my fault and that I somehow contrived to be naughty at every opportunity.

At one mealtime we were being supervised by Sister Stobard. She was a real dragon to me and she smoked like one, too. When we ate our meals, each of us had a blue rubber mat put under our plates, so that when we grabbed at our food with our mouths or stumps or sticks or whatever Heath Robinson extensions the workshop engineers had fitted us up with, the plates would not slide all over the table. For some reason, Sister Stobard decided to inspect the mats. Most likely some troublemaker had prodded her into doing it. When she got to me she picked up my plate and underneath it the blue rubber mat had a hole in the middle about the size of an orange. She held it up dramatically in front of my face and immediately accused me of deliberately making the hole by picking away at the rubber with my pincers. I agreed that somebody must have done it but it wasn't me. She didn't believe me. That was another thread of life, the way that the staff rarely believed us even if we were innocent of some charge or other. Although the staff had their favourites they still had the attitude that we children were always in the wrong. Naturally Sister Stobard's outstanding ability as a supervising nurse and purveyor of justice did not go unrewarded. She eventually became Head of Nursing.

Alban Block, the building where I lived, had two parts: an inner section and an outer section. The inner was warm and had central heating. It was where the more delicate types like the spina bifidas lived. And for us toughies, as we were called, there was the outer part, which didn't have heating and was freezing cold in winter. The toughies in the outer section were accommodated in large dormitories, twenty or thirty to a room, with our metal cots laid out in rows: cot, locker; cot, locker; cot, locker. Big cots with tall sides, so it was like being in a cage. I wasn't able to get out on my own. Somebody had to unlatch the side and let me out.

At night they used to put me inside my cot with the high sides, never in any underwear for some reason, just a little nightie, and in the morning they'd wake us at six o'clock, while it was still dark outside. The nurse would sweep through the dormitory in her starched uniform with her assistants tagging along behind her, making sure everyone woke up.

I had to wait my turn for the bathroom – there were up to thirty of us – so a nurse picked me up out of my bed and plonked me down on the floor. I remember the shock as my bare skin came up against the hard, freezing cold concrete. All around me cockroaches were running about but I didn't mind them as much as feeling my bottom and legs slowly going numb with the cold. Eventually someone would take me to the bathroom to wash my face and clean my teeth. After being dressed, it was off to breakfast, which we all took together in a huge refectory.

I didn't start going to school until I was five and so before that time I just used to play with my friends and my dolls. But our play could be interrupted by various other calls on our time, the most significant being the workshop visit.

About once a week a group of us would be taken to the workshops for a fitting. The priorities were rehabilitation and independence, which meant regular visits to the workshops across the road to be kitted out with artificial arms and legs. They wanted to normalise us. I can see that from an able-bodied person's point of view that is the logical thing to do. We would be piled into the large wooden cattle-truck trolleys and trundled along the connecting path by nursing assistants.

I always enjoyed going to the workshop. It was a great adventure and I didn't mind what it was for because it was a chance to meet somebody else, somebody new. We were all starved of social contact and didn't meet many other people so it was a treat to spend some time with the brown-coated, mechanical-engineering wizards in the workshop. They were all men who had obviously played very seriously with their Lego and Meccano sets when they were boys, and were still doing it, only now on a much larger scale. They were fully qualified engineers with HND certificates and thousands of hours training on lathes and saw benches and metal-cutting equipment. Their approach to the work was very steady, calm and patient, which I found quite a relief after the abrasive discipline of the dorm.

The workshop had a very easy-going atmosphere. The men who were there did not come from the nursing tradition of strictness, discipline and giving out a minimum of information. They were chatty and allowed us to do what we wanted while we waited to be seen. Their job was to design, build and then fit us into various kinds of limb-like constructions made from wood and steel. In part, the intention was to enable us to do the normal things that people in the outside world did, but they also wanted to help us to look as normal as possible.

It was an impressive process. During a series of repeat fittings, the workshop technicians spent many hours measuring my chest and torso and the circumference of my stumps and the width of my shoulders. I didn't mind at all. They were less prejudiced about us than most people because they lived in their world of mechanical engineering. We were not a blight on normal society to them but more like a physics problem which could be solved by the correct use of Newton's laws and the right raw materials. It was all very admirable but the final results, the awkward arm-substitutes, were ridiculous.

Well, I found them ridiculous, mainly because it was virtually impossible to use them for the purpose for which they were intended. The first ones I had were manually powered and I would have to use my shoulders to make them work by just swinging them about. At the end of each metal cylinder was a hook, rather like Captain Hook's but smaller. And the hooks were vicious and difficult to use. When I had them on I looked like a very badly made doll. It soon became apparent to all, even the sisters who could usually be relied on to stick with any system through thick and thin even if it didn't work, that the Mark I Artificial Arm had no useful future.

Undaunted, the workshop engineers set to work and I went in for more fittings over several months. The result of their cutting and grinding and filing and screwing together was the improved Mark II version. My new arms looked great. They were made of smooth metal and were powered by replaceable gas cylinders and, in fact, looked like something from a very low budget sci-fi movie from the 1950s. Unfortunately for all concerned, the Mark II arms were as uncontrollable and impossible to use as the Mark Is. My friends and I hardly ever used these artificial limbs for anything they were intended for and mostly just to fight each other or make holes in the tables. They were much more fun being used in that way.

They were very crude and largely ineffective contraptions which I hated using. Each arm was built into the shoulder socket and the whole arm was held on to my shoulder stump by leather cross-straps with small adjustable buckles. The cross-straps were fitted tightly across my chest so that the arms didn't slip off. If I moved a lever under my chin in one direction a pair of pincers would close shut at the end where my hand would have been. Moving the lever the other way would open the pincers. They had no sensitivity. They could only open and shut. When they closed on something that I wanted to pick up, they would totally crush it if it was anything other than metal or wood. And they opened with such a snap that I almost always dropped anything I was holding.

The staff were very keen that we all become proficient in the use of our artificial limbs. The add-on limbs were considered a fundamental aspect of our being able to function properly and fulfil the ultimate aim of the home: that we should be able to take care of ourselves. So when we were eating they always stood behind the tables and watched us to make sure we used them. They had great faith in those artificial limbs and thought that if we would only practise and use them regularly we would soon be picking up even the most delicate items without breaking or damaging them. But we all instinctively knew those sorry bits of metal were never going to fulfil their hoped-for potential.

My technique was to play with my food, nudging it round the plate and trying to look as if I was about to bring a portion up to my mouth. This was a long-winded operation. Although they provided a circular plastic guard round the plate so the food didn't go off the edge, when I approached a bit of something with my pincers it would just slip away, round and round in a circle at the edge of the plate. I'd keep moving it for a while, getting more and more frustrated. Then, when I thought nobody was looking, I would dive down and take a gulp of food with my mouth. Of course, I couldn't do that every time. Occasionally I would manage to push the lever under my chin in the right way at the right time and it would clamp on to a sliver of food, which it crushed flat. Even more rarely I managed to bring the crushed sliver up to my mouth and push the lever the other way just in time for the morsel to fall in. But for most of us, that ideal scenario of fluid and skilful adaptation to our artificial extensions never happened.

If a stranger had walked into our dining room during a typical mealtime they would have encountered the funniest slapstick routine unfolding in front their eyes. They would have seen some of us chasing the same bit of food round and round a plate without ever getting hold of it. I never managed to eat any of my meals hot for that reason. Others would have succeeded in grabbing a piece of something but then would whack themselves in the chin or eye when they tried to lift it up to their mouth. Yet others would accidentally flip their food down the table or across it into someone's lap or face. On one occasion, when my gas-powered arms were being particularly unruly, I managed to pick up and flick a full bowl of cornflakes and milk in a big arc over my head. When I looked behind me I saw that it had splattered against the window ten feet away and was slowly sliding down the glass. For a long time the nurses thought we were doing it on purpose.

It took a few years but by the time I was seven or eight the authorities had accepted that the experiment wasn't working and they more or less gave up asking us to use artificial arms. Instead a knife and spoon were strapped directly to my stumps.

It always amazes me when I see a disabled adult using a hook where their hand once was. I suppose the hook acts as a psychological substitute for the hand they once had. But I have never had hands or arms. I only know the body I have and a hook or anything else would be awkward and unnecessary.

To be fair to the workshop staff, not all their experiments were abject failures like the arms. They also made quite effective legs for Tara and myself – again after many months of measuring and adjustments – and, apart from the problem of chafing, they worked quite well. I used my artificial legs during all my time at the home and even after I left.

I had a real affection for the workshop engineers and I look back on the hours I spent with them as very pleasant memories. I think what would really have helped all of us would have been something none of the adults at the home could bring themselves to do: listen to what we had to say and try out some of our ideas as well as their own. We were the ones with the direct experience of how our limb-deficient bodies worked and understood best how to use our bodies to do the things they wanted us to learn how to do. I wish they had asked us what we thought at the beginning. By the time I was ten, the process became much more of a collaboration and the results far more impressive.

3

Norfolk Days

*F*or the first two and a half years of my life, I think I may have been one of the few children who didn't go home during the holidays. We had holiday breaks at the usual times of Christmas, Easter and during the summer, and most of the children would go home to their families. I have been told that I did have some visitors called the Hutts who took me home for the weekend when I was very little. But they went to America and my occasional trips out came to a halt. I don't have any memory of that time so I can't say whether I felt upset about being left behind. I do know that I wanted to go out with someone like the other children did.

At the age of two I still had not been fitted with artificial legs and moved about by sliding along on my bottom. A new nurse, Susannah Child, had arrived at the home and was working on Alban Block. She was warmer and more approachable than the other nurses and I took to following her about as she did her duties. She noticed me and, although I was a very quiet child at that time, she seemed to enjoy my company and gave me a bit more of her attention than was required by her duties.

The other children were being visited by their parents and taken out for the day, or for the weekend, or even for longer periods if it was the holidays. I wanted to be taken out, too, so I shuffled after Sister Child one day and asked her if I could go out with her. She said that I couldn't because she wasn't an official visitor and that it was against the rules for staff to take out children. I was disappointed but resigned, and assumed I would only be able to see Sister Child when she was at work. In the meantime she must have worked hard at persuading the authorities to let her take me out. They must have relented because one day she asked me if I'd like to go to tea with her. We only went as far as one of the caravans provided on the site for parents who were making an overnight visit, but it was as good as a holiday as far as I was concerned. Soon Sister Child was taking me further afield on little shopping expeditions.

One shop owner was so taken with me that she gave me a rag doll which I promptly christened Esmeralda. Sister Child also bought me dresses and a beautiful little cape, but I was unable to keep any of those items for myself. The home had a system where all the toys and clothes any of the children returned with were put into a communal pool. My Esmeralda became a general toy for anyone and the cape was given to another girl. There was nobody there who could confirm that this item or that item belonged to a particular child. The staff apportioned everything from the pool as they saw fit, so we had very few personal possessions.

Sister Child shared a house with the deputy matron, Jean Tate, and after a while I began to visit them there for tea. They must have liked me because when they booked a ten-day summer holiday for themselves on the Norfolk Broads they asked me if I'd like to go with them. Of course I said yes.

We drove to Norfolk and arrived at the mooring where we were to board our hire craft. I had never seen a boat up close before and when I saw this one I didn't like the idea of stepping aboard. The way it moved in the water looked too unsafe, so I asked my two nurses if we could stay in the car and drive that on the water instead. They looked at each other and laughed. Susannah tried to explain to me why it was impossible for cars to travel on water and that we would all sink if we tried it. After that they managed to coax me on to the boat and, once we got moving, I fell in love with the motion and the smooth way we were gliding through the still water. One of the first craft we met was an amphibious car. There were probably only about three of them in the whole of Britain but it happened to be cruising by on my first day in a boat. I looked at the nurses accusingly but they just laughed. They explained to me how rare such cars were but I was convinced that I had been right all along.

One sunny day followed another. Sometimes the two

nurses cooked a meal on board in the tiny galley and sometimes we went ashore to a pub or a restaurant.

At the end of the ten days Jean took us to visit her
mother at her little cottage on a farm which belonged to her
son, Colin. Jean's other brother in Norfolk, Hilton, lived in
the village of Colkirk with his wife, Daphne, and their two
boys, Simon and Vernon. I met Daphne, Hilton and the boys
in Colin's farmhouse kitchen and I immediately took to them
and they to me. Hilton showed me round the farm. I saw
turkeys and pigs and cows for the first time. And then, far
too soon, it was time to return for the Christmas term at the
home.

In the meantime, Susannah and Jean had seen how well I
had got on with the Tates and had an idea. Jean telephoned
Hilton and Daphne and asked if they would be prepared to
have me for a week during the coming Christmas holidays. I
knew the Tates had taken to me but they were also the sort of
people who believed in behaving decently and doing the right
thing. They felt a lot of sympathy for my situation as
described to them by Jean and I don't think it took much per-
suasion for them to agree to have me in their home for
Christmas. Any concerns they might have had about looking
after me were allayed by the fact that Jean and Susannah, both
nurses, would be staying nearby at Colin's farm. If any problems occurred, Jean and Susannah would be on hand to help
deal with them.

I didn't know it at the time but with three days left
before the Christmas holidays the Hutts reappeared. They
had returned from their extended stay in America and wanted

to have me with them for Christmas, and because they had been the first visitors to take me out the social worker thought they should have preference over the Tates. Susannah made a fervent last-minute plea to the authorities. Arrangements were already made. The Tates and their children were looking forward to my arrival. We had got on well with each other when we met in the summer and it would be a shame to change all the plans at the last minute, especially as Simon and Vernon would be disappointed. The authorities found in favour of the Tates and the Hutts retired gracefully from the scene.

A few days before the Christmas break in 1967 Jean came to see me in the playroom of my dorm and asked me whether I'd like to go to the Tate family for Christmas instead of staying at the home. She was very reassuring. She said that they would take good care of me, that there would be Simon and Vernon for me to play with, and that there would be Christmas presents. I would like to say that I immediately jumped at the chance to spend Christmas away. Certainly that would normally have been the case, but I suddenly felt shy about spending a week in someone else's home, especially as I didn't know them well. Jean said that I could think about it and that nobody was forcing me to go. And when she said that I knew I would say yes.

I waited impatiently for her to come to see me the next day so that I could tell her that I wanted to go. I was afraid that because I hadn't said yes straightaway her offer might be withdrawn. But when I told her that I wanted to go she seemed very pleased, almost more so than I was. I think she didn't want me to say no after all the arrangements she'd made, but also I think she felt sorry for my situation and wanted me to have a real family Christmas just as other people did.

Once I got it into my head that I was going to spend Christmas with a family who lived a long way away, I got more and more excited as the days went by. I packed and repacked my tiny little suitcase with my few clothes and finally the actual day arrived. Jean and Susannah put me in Jean's car and we drove all the way to Colkirk. Unfortunately, I didn't travel well in cars when I was little and was sick on the back seat. Jean and Susannah didn't seem to mind. They were both in high spirits because it was the Christmas holidays and they were getting a break from the home – just as I was.

The Tates lived in a cul-de-sac in a large three-bedroom bungalow. We turned into their big shingle drive and Jean switched off the engine. I was very quiet, overcome by a sudden shyness. Jean picked me up and carried me into the house, while Susannah followed with my little case. We went into the kitchen for a cup of tea and Hilton and Daphne and Vernon and Simon gave me a very warm welcome. I knew immediately that I was going to be very happy staying with them for Christmas.

After the tea (we drank a lot of tea at the Tates), they took me to my room where they had prepared a cot for me to sleep in. Daphne laid out my clothes on a little low table while I looked round the room. For the first time, I would be sleeping in a room of my own.

Before long it was time for supper, which Daphne laid out

on two tables. I ate with the boys. We had our own low coffee table with three little stools and we sat in a circle enjoying supper in our little corner café. The boys ate with their hands and I ate with my feet. Daphne and Hilton had their meal next to us at a full-size table more suited to their height. It was a very good arrangement and I liked eating with the boys in our little corner. I have to say, Simon and Vernon were very accepting of me from the first moment of our meeting. They never made comments about my lack of arms or teased me in any way. They were aged two and four and perhaps children as young as that have yet to develop any prejudice, but I think also that Simon and Vernon just happened to be two very nice boys with two very nice parents.

I settled in with the Tate family without any problems and soon felt at home there. On Christmas morning I woke up full of excitement. At the end of my cot was a big Santa's sack full of toys. Daphne and the boys were in the doorway where they had been waiting for me to wake up. She picked me up, together with my sack of toys, and we skipped along to Hilton and Daphne's bedroom and got into their bed. There were five of us squashed in together but it didn't seem to matter. Simon and Vernon and I pulled out our Christmas stocking fillers one by one and unwrapped them while Daphne and Hilton looked on. It's hard to describe the feelings I had. I was so loved and welcomed and accepted into this family that I felt as if I were truly one of them myself. I was one of the Tate children enjoying a Christmas at home in the most natural way.

We had breakfast next, with cups of tea, and then all of us went to the Christmas tree in the front room to look for our presents. The Tates had bought me a beautiful painted rocking horse and Susannah's present to me was a lovely red doll's house. I was thrilled. I couldn't decide whether to ride my horse or play with my doll's house. They were both so appealing.

My second visit to Norfolk soon came to an end and I was back at the home thinking about the next time I would be visiting the Tates. They had asked me if I would like to come back for the Easter holidays and I replied that, of course, I would. Jean kept me informed about the dates and soon enough Easter came and I was on my way once again to my new home. But the arrangements were a little different for my third holiday in Norfolk. Jean and Susannah would not becoming this time. They took me to Liverpool Street and Hilton met us there. In addition, I had by now become the proud owner of a pair of artificial legs and a pair of the artificial gas-powered arms. These were packed away in a special bulky case of their own. I also took the case which contained my clothes and toys.

When we arrived at Norwich station Hilton put me under one arm and, with the two cases under his other arm and our tickets in his mouth, strode down the platform to the exit where Daphne and the boys were waiting for us. It was wonderful to be back and as the days passed I became more and more accustomed to being part of the family. The boys always called Daphne Mummy and one day I asked her if I could call her that, too. She said yes I could and from then on Daphne was mummy to me.

I loved being with the Tates and they seemed to love me

being there, too. I was treated no differently to Simon and Vernon, and gradually the idea took hold that they really were my brothers. When the boys and I played together, I found that I could make up for some of the advantages they had from their extra mobility by using my gas-powered pincers to nip them during games of chase.

I couldn't walk at all at that time but I was meant to practise with my artificial legs for a few hours every morning. Daphne religiously, bless her, knowing I hated it, strapped me into my fibreglass legs after breakfast and I would try walking on their garden lawn, with Daphne there to catch me if I fell over. The staff had told her that it was very important for me to practise with my legs and she took their request very seriously. However, by the time I had my legs and arms strapped on I was more or less as stiff as a board and found it very hard to move, let alone walk.

One day we thought it would be good to practise my walking out on the driveway because it had a different surface to what I was used to. I was in my legs but was finding it very hard to keep my balance on the slippery gravel. Because I had no arms, if I lost my balance and toppled over I would be completely unable to break my fall. I would just land with a smash, my face hitting the gravel with the rest of my body. Daphne decided my wild skids and wobblings were getting too dangerous so she picked me up and carried me back into the house through the front door. She asked me what I wanted to do next and I said play in the kitchen, so she moved towards the open kitchen doorway. There was a step up with a lip on it and as she tried to lift me over it my feet got caught on the lip.

Daphne screamed and fell awkwardly as she tried to make sure that I wasn't hurt by the fall. She badly gashed her knee and there was blood everywhere. I remember Hilton saying that the wound would have to be stitched up and I imagined that that must be the worst possible thing. I felt guilty about it, even at three years old. It was all my fault. Of course, she was lovely about it even though she was in pain. I remember her leg was 'bad' for a long time. It was a constant reminder that I'd hurt her somehow. I don't suppose she'd see it like that at all. But I did. Guilt was always lurking there, ready to spring into any situation and confirm that I was somehow as 'wrong' inside as I looked to others on the outside.

My best visits to Norfolk were in the summer. Hilton's brother, Colin, had a farm with 140 acres of land. They had eighty Friesian dairy cows and some sheep and ducks, and turkeys for Christmas. Hilton worked there, too, looking after the cows while Colin concentrated on the wheat and barley crops. At the end of the day Daphne took the boys and me up to the farm and we would join Hilton in the milking parlour while he milked the cows. I remember being lifted up to stroke a cow, astonished by its huge head and big brown eyes. If you're wondering how I was able to stroke animals when I had no arms and hands the answer is simple: I used my feet. I was fascinated by the farm animals because I had only ever seen cats and dogs at the home.

Life was quiet but very pleasant in Colkirk. We went for walks and little shopping expeditions, sometimes in the village and sometimes further away to Dereham. I never wore my artificial legs on these trips and as I couldn't walk on my own

Daphne pushed me along in a pushchair. We met many of the Tates' fellow villagers and neighbours. They were all curious and interested in my condition but they never made any unpleasant remarks or showed any sign of distaste in their expressions.

One lady we met, Mrs Smith, was the wife of a Salvation Army general. The Tates must have told her all about me and had probably mentioned that I didn't have many clothes. Mrs Smith responded by making me a dress. It was a very detailed crochet garment which must have taken her several days of work. From then on, every time I visited Norfolk and we went to see her there would be another new dress waiting for me. But, as always, they went into the pool of clothes when I got back to the home.

Occasionally we went on an expedition which was more out of the ordinary. I remember all of us going on the Norfolk Broads for the day. I loved the way the stately craft slipped smoothly through the water. As we drifted sedately along I saw ducks and swans as well as the much smaller creatures who made their homes in the riverbank.

However, the best part of my summer visits was the harvest picnics. At harvest time Colin started up the combine harvester very early in the morning and it rumbled up and down the wheat fields reaping the grain. A little while later Colin's wife, Phyllis, would drive up on a tractor with a trailer on the back and take all the grain from the combine back to the barn by the farmhouse. After lunch, Daphne, the boys and I would come and watch the last part of the harvest, which was making the straw bails. At about four o'clock everyone stopped working and we gathered round to form a small circle in the stubble. Hilton and Daphne, Colin and Phyllis and their children, the boys and I, and a couple of the farm labourers opened our freshly made packets of sandwiches and tea was poured for everyone from the big flasks Daphne had brought. The sun was still shining but the hard work of the day was over. I couldn't wear my legs in the stubble because I would have fallen over with my first step. So I just sat and ate my sandwiches and drank my tea and watched the boys playing on the bales of straw. It was very simple when I think about it now but there was a lovely atmosphere of togetherness and I loved being part of that.

The next holiday was to be my second Christmas with the Tate family. Again, Jean and Susannah took me as far as London and Hilton came down in his car and brought me the rest of the way to Colkirk. There were smiles and hugs and I experienced my usual feeling of coming home again. I felt more secure and at ease with them than ever.

Daphne's mother was an organist at the church in Brisby and she ran a Sunday school there. On Sundays, Simon and Vernon attended the Sunday school and, when I was staying with the Tates, so did I. As it was Christmas the church was putting on a nativity play in which the boys were taking part. I went along to the church to see the rehearsals and I was asked if I would like to be in it, too. I said yes without any hesitation. I didn't care what part I was going to play as long as I could be up on stage with the other children. Nevertheless I was pleased when I discovered that I was to play one of the angels. Angels do look so cute. Daphne rustled up a sweet little costume for me, like a white smock, and, of course, I had beautiful white wings attached to my shoulders. Hilton says I was a regular little showgirl. I beamed with pleasure and took to being on stage as if I was born to it.

Later in the holiday they took me and the boys to see *Aladdin*, my first pantomime, in Dereham. Hilton was playing the part of the Evil Ebenezar and I remember him terrorizing Aladdin in his cave while singing 'If I Were a Rich Man'. I loved the show with its melodramatic style and audience participation. Towards the end of the performance all the children in the audience joined the cast on stage for a sing-along. Hilton took the boys up and one of his friends, the best man at his wedding, came and found me in my seat and took me up as well. Once again I found myself on stage and thoroughly enjoying it. I realize that I'm describing those holidays with the Tates as an idyllic time where I enjoyed every day and nothing horrible ever happened. But that is how I remember it and I think that is probably how it was.

I was coming up to my fourth birthday in the spring and had been visiting the Tates since I was two and a half. I was completely settled in with them and they were very comfortable with having me. So much so that they made enquiries with the authorities, through Jean, to find out what they would have to do to adopt me. I'm quite sure that they saw me as part of their family and loved me as one of their own.

I don't think the authorities at the home had any objection. They knew that my mother had given me up at birth and had made no contact to find out how I was getting on. I didn't receive Christmas or birthday cards from her or from any of my relatives in Birmingham. So the authorities probably assumed that there would be no objection to the Tates adopting me. They knew that the Tates looked after me well, cared about me and that my holiday visits to Norfolk had been a great success all round. There could be no reason why I shouldn't be adopted by them and become sister to Simon and Vernon. Of course, they would have to contact my mother because she would be required to sign the adoption papers.

If my mother had signed those papers I would have gone to live in Norfolk with the Tates. My name would be Alison Tate today and I would have had a very different life. But instead of being adopted and leaving the home, my visits to Norfolk suddenly came to an end. I had no idea why at the time. I wasn't given a reason, so I just cried to myself and wondered where the Tates had gone. Why weren't they coming to see me any more? I assumed I'd done something terrible to offend them and they didn't want anything more to do with me. I didn't see the Tates again until I was in my twenties and years later I found out that my mother had stopped the adoption. For some reason that I cannot fathom she chose that moment to step back into my life.

It was a day like any other, a Saturday, and I was crawling about with my friends inside my residential block. Our playroom was on the ground floor and looked out through French doors on to a concrete courtyard with a grass bank at the end of it. Sitting on the grass were a group of people I'd never seen before. Me and my friends were all looking over in their direction and wondering who they were. The next thing I knew a staff member came through the doors and, without a word, picked me up. I had no idea what was going on. Maybe she was taking me to the medical wing for an examination by some visiting doctors' group or maybe they needed me in the workshops to take some more measurements for my artificial limbs. But I knew almost immediately that we weren't going in the right direction for either of those. She was taking me directly towards the sloping bank and the group of strangers.

'These are your parents.'

'No, they're not. She's not my mum. She doesn't look anything like my mum.'

The Tates were my parents. I refused to speak any more and promptly slid down the bank, scrabbling away as fast and as far as I could. The nurse immediately caught up with me, picked me up and dumped me once more next to the group we had been discussing moments earlier. My heart was pounding but my body was frozen in panic. I somehow knew this sudden awkward meeting was going to have huge implications for my life. And I didn't like it at all.

No explanation. No coaching or counselling. Nobody to say: 'Don't worry, it'll be all right.' I was supposed to believe that these people who had sprung from nowhere were my parents. Just like that. Well, I didn't believe it. They all spoke funnily for one thing. I'd spent my whole life in the South and had never heard a Brummie accent. So there I was, aged four, being handed over to a bunch of complete strangers with odd accents, who were about to remove me from the place I called home. I was completely stunned. The strangers were, in fact, my two grandparents, my sister, Vanessa, and my mother with her new husband, my stepfather, Alan.

They put me in their car and took me to Birmingham. I

spent the whole journey petrified. I kept asking where I was going, where they were taking me. They probably said Birmingham but that word didn't mean anything to me. Eventually we arrived. My mother and stepfather lived at the very top of a council high-rise building, on the thirteenth floor. The top two floors housed the lift mechanism so they had to carry me up the stairs for the last bit of the journey. I was brought into their small two-bedroom flat and put down on the floor. I was still in shock and couldn't take it in, but Vanessa, my sister, took me into her bedroom, which I was to share with her. She took me under her wing in a very natural and kindly way, showing me her things and unpacking mine. I was fascinated by her – by the fact that I had a sister – and I happily allowed myself to be cocooned by her kindness and protection.

It was a different thing with my mother. I noticed a coldness emanating from her, as if I was an unfortunate inconvenience in her life, and I remember lying in bed feeling very confused. I realized that these strangers were my actual family and that I would have to get used to that, but for some reason I didn't feel the warmth and security and love that I had experienced in Norfolk with the Tates.

4

Mummy Dearest

*M*y mother. Where do I start? We've never talked about anything properly so I don't really know how she felt. This is
how a social worker described our relationship in a report:

> Alison was admitted when she was a few weeks old, with
> the history that she had been totally rejected by her
> mother. It was not until Alison was four years old that the
> Social Worker approached her remarried mother, Mrs
> Barber, in Birmingham and some contact was made.
> Although Alison spent holidays with her mother and
> step-father when she was a child, the relationship was
> not easy. Mrs Barber had only limited affection for

Alison, which was described as a certain admiration mixed with pity and revulsion.

I think that's pretty clear, don't you?

My mother, Veronica Barber, comes from a working-class family in Birmingham and was brought up by her parents with two brothers, both younger than her. Her father was a left-wing city councillor and union official from the days when you didn't receive any money for holding either position. He was an old-fashioned man, far from rich, who believed in his principles and lived by them. In later life when he had a chance to buy the council house that he lived in he refused to do so. He didn't think it was right. I think all three children had a typical childhood of moderate working-class deprivation. They always had enough for their basic needs but there were few luxuries in the house.

My mother left school at fifteen and worked in the Lucas car components factory as a machinist. I sometimes find it hard to imagine her working in a factory but I suppose it was necessary for her to have a job and the Lucas works was a major employer in the area. Many of her friends would have been working there as well.

She doesn't look like a factory worker, more like a beautician or hairdresser, and she takes a lot of care with her appearance. 'I'd rather go out without my knickers on than without my make-up' is one of her sayings. She takes longer to apply her make-up than I do, which is saying something. She is an attractive woman, a brunette with a huge head of fine hair and an hourglass figure. My friends who met her always remember her hair piled up on top of her head in a magnificent beehive style. It must have taken hours for the hairdresser to shampoo her hair and tease it into that spectacular shape.

She is soft and vivacious with men, and enjoys being the centre of their attention, particularly on social occasions. She can also be very hard, like her mother had been to her when I was born, but in spite of her steely interior and glamorous exterior she has never been very ambitious for herself in terms of having a high-flying career or making a lot of money. Her younger brother, my Uncle Nick, who I get on with like a house on fire, is an energetic go-getter with a big house and several businesses. But my mother is quite happy to stay in the two-bedroom council house that she moved to from the high-rise flat. Of course, the inside of the house is perfectly decorated in a slightly glittery and overdone style. You know the sort of thing – every tissue box must have an ornate lacy cover and nothing must ever be out of place.

Not long after I was born, she married Alan Barber, a mechanical engineer, and as far as I can tell they are absolutely devoted to each other. I am very fond of Alan. When I started to visit them in Birmingham during the holidays I began to call him Dad and I still call him that today. He is a very patient man. I only ever saw him get impatient when we were waiting in the hallway to go out and my mother was still applying her lipstick and perfume. We always seemed to be standing there for hours, waiting for her to sweep down the narrow stairs in all her finery. Alan is proud of me and I can tell that he cares about me. He bounced me on his knee and whooshed me up in the air like all dads do when their children are toddlers. I loved it and I loved his attention.

I don't recollect that my mother ever held me or sat me on her lap or did any of those tender things a mother might do with her child. I never understood it. She doted on my elder sister so she was quite capable of love and affection. I suppose she was so concerned with appearances and what people might think that my disabilities were just too much for her. She would look at me sometimes, in a certain way, and that look of hers would pierce me to my core. I can't describe it exactly. It felt to me that it was a mixture of so many things: disappointment, anger, pity, revulsion and something lurking there that was almost affection but not quite. I saw that look often. It seemed to say that I was a thorn in her side that she could never remove.

I've tried hard to imagine what it must have been like for her, having misshapen little Alison as her daughter, and I can understand that it was not easy. She had never received any counselling or professional advice that might have helped her come to terms with my birth. And it must have been very uncomfortable for her to keep all her feelings and thoughts about me hidden and shut down. I have no doubt that she felt partly to blame for the way my body was, even though it can't be considered her fault in any way. I don't think she knew how to deal with the guilt and pain she must have felt when I was born, and, perhaps inevitably, she coped with all her mental turmoil by transferring some of her self-blaming to blaming me instead. It would have been so much easier if I just hadn't existed or had died after a few days like the people in the hospital said I would.

Instead, she allowed the hospital authorities to take me away somewhere, never to be seen again. And I was her child. I would think that's a very heavy decision for a mother to have to live with. For my part I have tortured myself with the thought that she didn't absolutely *have* to give me up the way that she did. She could have insisted on seeing me when I was born. She could have insisted on knowing where they were taking me and she could have insisted on being allowed to see how I was getting on when I was a baby at the home. But perhaps she couldn't. Things were different then. And sadly for both of us that bit of our past can't ever be changed.

The person I became closest to in Birmingham was my sister Vanessa – Nessie. She and my mother had very similar tastes, all pinks and purples and prettiness, but she didn't have the complicated view of me that my mother had. She was much closer to my age, of course, and much easier to get to know. When I came to stay I was given a little put-you-up bed in the corner of Nessie's room, and a drawer with some clothes and a few toys. I also had a little step to use in the bathroom, which my mother hated because it spoiled the carefully designed decor. She maintained an underlying level of disapproval of me which never went away and meant that I always felt like a visitor in the house.

But Nessie was very nice to me and I felt much safer and happier in her company. She involved me in her life and took me out to places like the park and the swimming pool. On these trips to the outside world she and I received glances and the occasional cutting remark, but Nessie seemed to take them in her stride and always defended me if people behaved callously. She made me feel that I was special to her, that I really *was* her sister.

I would watch her in the bath and look at her doing her make-up. Before she did her own, she used to show me how I could apply lipstick and eyeliner myself. And she used to paint little forget-me-nots in the corner of my eyes. I loved her and admired her and looked up to her. She was my friend. And she cared.

During my early time at the home I had had a grumbling appendix but it had never been diagnosed as such. One Christmas holiday, when I was seven years old, my stomach began to hurt again. I tried to put up with it as best I could but the pain got worse and worse. By Christmas Eve I was vomiting every ten minutes. Neither my mother nor Alan got up to take care of me. It was Nessie who looked after me during that long night of endless vomiting. I was lying in bed hoping the pain would get better, but it didn't and soon a wave of nausea would hit me and I would moan: 'Nessie!' Straightaway she helped me out of bed and got me to the toilet so that I could be sick. After a while there seemed to be no point in getting back into bed each time so she just held me over the toilet all night. She was fully supporting my weight and her back must have been killing her but she never lost her patience with me. She just held me and kept telling me that everything would be all right. She was totally brilliant.

I don't know why my mother and Alan didn't take turns with Nessie, but they didn't. They probably didn't realise the seriousness of the medical situation. Eventually they did call the doctor, who came to the house. My appendix had ruptured during the night and peritonitis had set in. It was still in its early stages and was dealt with without becoming life-threatening.

The whole incident shows the difference between Nessie's relationship with me and the one I had with my parents. She did things for me at home that nobody else ever did and I still love her for that. She was the person I looked forward to seeing when I went home for the holidays because we did things together. We had girly evenings and practised our make-up and only occasionally did she get irritated by my endless little girl questions. As she got older and started going out with boyfriends, I saw less of Nessie. When she got ready for one of her evenings out I would try to delay her for as long as possible but, although she was as friendly and loving as she had always been with me, her interests were elsewhere.

When she was nineteen she became pregnant, married the father of her child, and left home. It was a major blow for me because Nessie was no longer there when I came to Birmingham for the holidays. Now there was only Alan and my mother to come home to. He was working as an engineer doing the night shift in a local factory. By the time I woke up in the mornings he had finished work and was fast asleep. My mother had left for the morning shift at Lucas's. She left me a bowl of cornflakes but because the milk had been added one or two hours earlier it was pretty soggy by the time I got to it. As the kitchen table was too high for me my cereal bowl was left on the floor and, more often than not, the cat got to it before I did. After breakfast I read the newspaper – they always got the *Sun* – and crept around the house so as not to wake Alan. If I desperately needed to go to the toilet then I would have to wake him up to help me because there was no one else in the house. I generally spent the morning watching television with the volume turned down very low. I remember being very lonely and bored. I had no friends and my parents didn't have a lot of time for me.

At lunchtime my mother would return from her factory shift and make us both lunch, usually a sandwich or something like that. If it was summer she would strip down to her bra, cover herself in suntan oil and lie down in the garden to get a tan. I would sit myself nearby and play with my dolls, hoping all the while that she would talk to me, but she hardly ever did. I was a little scared to disturb her so there was no conversation. Years later when I talked to her about it she lay the blame very firmly at my door: 'You never said anything, Alison.'

She appeared to me as a very remote, almost alien creature, always off to the hairdresser's. On one occasion Alan was up in the afternoon and we were in the back garden together. My mother left through the back gate with her hair piled up in all its brunette glory. Two hours later a statuesque blonde came back in through the same gate. Although she was wearing the same dress as my mother I simply didn't recognize her. Even when she spoke, the change in her appearance had been so dramatic that I couldn't put two and two together, and it took me about half an hour to realize that it really was her.

On a Friday or Saturday things cheered up a little. It was the weekend and Alan would go to the 'Outhouse', which is what they called the corner shop, and buy crisps and sweets.

Then we would curl up on the sofa and spend the evening watching television, programme after programme, while we ate the chips and stuffed ourselves with as many sweets as we wanted. I would sit next to Alan, not my mother, and he would hold my foot as if he were holding my hand. That was his sweet side, his saving grace as far as I was concerned. They allowed me to stay up watching television as late as they did and then it was off to bed. When Nessie had been at home she always read me a story at bedtime but my parents never did. It was just teeth, bed, lights out, 'Good night.'

I could never understand what it was about me that displeased my mother. Apart from the lack of limbs, I mean. I know she found the various accessories that I needed very irritating and she made it clear to the authorities that I was only to bring one small suitcase when I came home. I think she felt they were ugly and cluttered up the house. But I needed them. And the staff at the home considered it imperative that we become skilled in their use. They wanted us to be able to look after ourselves, to function. So like any other child I had to learn to dress myself.

The first thing I used was a wooden stand like an easel. It had two projecting wooden rods covered in pimple rubber, each about 4 inches long and 20 inches apart. I would spread open my pants with my feet and then use my mouth to hook them over the two rods. The pimple rubber kept them in place and I would step into them and wriggle around to get them on. For T-shirts or blouses I would do the same thing – stretch them across the two rods and then do a kind of head dive into the neck hole.

It was a very long process of learning how to do it, which took years. I used to practise before breakfast and it was an extremely frustrating time. I was often in tears because even after twenty minutes of sweaty effort I often failed to put on any clothes at all. After a few years the easel with the protruding rods was replaced by hooks screwed into the wall. Except that my mother refused to put them up because they were unsightly.

And later still, Peter Tutt, one of the engineers who designed everything I used, made me a pair of dressing sticks. They were made from hinged aluminium and had a hook at the end which I used to pull clothes on to myself. These were excellent because it meant I could take them with me wherever I went. But because I had to use them with my mouth they put a strain on my neck. I would have to twist my head almost 180 degrees to pull my trousers over my bottom. Now, thirty years later, both my back and neck are giving me a lot of trouble.

After Nessie left home I hardly ever went out of the house except for visits to family or the occasional friend. The three of us never went out by ourselves just for the fun of it; to visit the seaside or a funfair. I knew they took holidays, often abroad, but they always scheduled them to coincide with the time that I was back at the institution. When I went home for my holiday breaks they would bring out their holiday snaps and show me the places that they and Nessie had been to. They told me what a wonderful time they had and although they may have been completely oblivious to the effect it had on me, I felt hurt and left out.

From time to time a social worker would visit me and my parents at home to see how we were getting on. I think they knew that something wasn't quite right about my family life but they could never resolve what to do about it. My mother was good at stonewalling them. Here are some extracts from a social worker's report made in 1977 when I was twelve. Nessie had already left home.

I find it quite difficult to put down what I really feel about this visit . . . The terraced house is small, well kept and expensively furnished, with nothing out of place, in fact it hardly looks lived in. I now see why Alison does not wear her prostheses at home, partly because of the structural layout of the house, partly because she spends a great deal of time on her own, and partly because her mother finds them inconvenient and unsightly.

Alison does not seem to go out anywhere except in the car, and that doesn't seem often. I suggested that Alison might go and choose her own books in the local library but her mother implied that Alison never opened a book and that she had a lot of books of her own and that she would buy her any she wanted.

She eats her meals on the floor, and the cat sometimes gets at her food. Alison is puzzled about how to please her parents. If she asks permission to do something she's told 'You don't have to ask, it's your home.' But if she doesn't ask she gets told off.

That last part about asking permission is very characteristic of how my mother often dealt with me. It was damned if you do and damned if you don't.

My mother also had to give permission if special visitors wanted to take me out or have me in their homes for the weekend. I always enjoyed being taken out during term time because my parents very rarely came down. When I went home in the holidays I used to talk about it and describe the places I had been taken to and what a nice time I had had going out with this or that person.

Years later, a social worker confessed to me that when I was effusive in my praise of a particular visitor, my mother would get in touch with the authorities and ask them to stop letting me go out with that person. I never knew anything about it. I always assumed that I must have said or done something to upset them and that was the reason they severed their connection with me. I grew up feeling there must be something very wrong with me because of the way people disappeared from my life. If I had known that that was what was happening I would never have said anything to my parents when I went home in the holidays. The only visitor I had who was not forbidden was a lady called Jackie, who used to take me out when I was fifteen. I didn't talk about Jackie when I was at home.

Looking back now, I wonder if my mother signed permissions for operations to be carried out without really considering the implications. I suppose she assumed the doctors knew what they were doing, but I think some of their work, intended to shape me better for using prosthetics, was unnecessary. Now I have a scar down to my breast on my left side.

When I was sixteen I began to try to talk to my mother about my birth. I was always intensely curious about my disability and I still am. I have talked to a geneticist about it and all he could tell me was that he didn't know. Normally a body such as mine would be aborted by a miscarriage. So why did I get through? It's a kind of miracle and I must have wanted to live very badly. I've never been angry about it, but I wanted some kind of explanation. I wanted to understand the circumstances better and get some answers to the questions I had wrestled with all my life. What had happened when I was born? Why had she allowed me to be sent to the home? Why was I there for so long before she brought me back? But she seemed to find it very difficult to discuss her feelings and talk about what had happened. I wanted to know as much as possible so that I could understand why she had allowed me to be taken from her and why her attitude to me had always been so cold. Her response was to blame everyone else involved. She always maintained that other people were at fault, not herself. She has strict control over her own emotions in that suppressed English way and she used to dislike me crying or being emotional as well. She can't cope with the emotional side of life at all. She has taken the events surrounding my birth and adjusted them to the shape that is the least threatening to her peace of mind. Some of her adjustments are simply a matter of adopting a view that leaves her with the least pain and guilt. In addition, she sometimes alters the facts.

One of the most important adjustments of fact only

emerged when I began writing this book. I wanted to accumulate as much research material as possible and had applied to the local authority archives for them to release all the documents relating to me from my time at the institution. They told me that all the documents had been lost, but I refused to accept that and kept asking different departments whether there might be any papers that perhaps had been kept in some other place. Eventually, some months later, over a hundred A4 pages were unearthed and I had a full set of copies sent to me.

The large manila envelope was waiting for me when I got home one day from a visit to London. I saw it lying on the mat just inside the door and was suddenly overcome with an intense feeling of dread and uncertainty. What was going to be revealed in those pages of scribbled text? They had been written by people confidentially. Everything that was said was meant to be kept secret from me, the subject.

I went into my front room and sat down on my favourite recliner with a cup of tea. I was feeling the need to gather myself together, to steel myself. A friend of mine was visiting that day. He had opened the envelope for me and placed the contents on a small glass-topped table. I took long sips of tea through my straw and looked at the fat pile of white photocopy paper sitting in front of me. We joked for a while about what we might find in the writing: lurid revelations of some kind or pages of boring notes with nothing interesting in them at all. I kept sipping my tea but after ten minutes I lost my hesitancy and picked up the first sheet.

It didn't say much. It was the social services department

admission form written up when I was shipped to the home at six weeks old. My eyes ran over the typewritten entries in a cursory way. I was not expecting a standard document like this to reveal anything of interest. There was my name, date of birth, nationality and place of birth – all the usual stuff. Halfway down the paper was a section headed: Family. Suddenly my eyes went wide when I saw the entries:

Father: George Morton, 32, coach driver
Mother: Veronica Lapper, 29, machinist
Others: Vanessa, 8
Father was in the Navy from 16 years of age until 24 years (address not known)

'Oh my God!'
'What is it?'
'Look at this.'

While my friend read the one-page document I could feel my chest tighten and my head go slightly dizzy. All my life I had believed what my mother had told me: that Vanessa and I had the same father, Gordon Lapper. And I had spent thirty-nine years of my life with the surname Lapper assuming it was my father's name. Suddenly all that blighted but comforting history was gone. It was all a lie. But I still couldn't quite believe the truth. I took the document back and kept reading and rereading the few typewritten words. I was finding it hard to take in, to accept. Why did my mother keep the truth from me all these years?

I assumed she must have had an affair with somebody

called George Morton and become pregnant with me. It would have been too complicated and shameful in those days to tell the world at large the truth. And as the years went by it became easier and easier to stick to the story that I was the daughter of Gordon Lapper, father of Nessie. But that was back then. Values had changed. There was a new realization that it wasn't healthy to suppress the truth and keep secrets. Not least because secrets have a way of getting out in the end. So why didn't you tell me the truth, Ma?

I was experiencing all kinds of feelings including anger, shock, dismay and even a little relief to know the truth at last. But underlying all of those was the one word that had always haunted me and coloured my feelings about my mother: betrayal. I reviewed in my mind our long history as mother and daughter. What had I done? Was my behaviour so bad that all the problems we had should be laid at my door? I didn't think so. I had always tried as hard as I could to be what I thought she wanted me to be. I wanted her to be happy with me but she never was. I could never get it right, the job of being her daughter. Even on occasions like my birthday my mother's dissatisfaction would express itself. The birthdays I spent at home were nothing special. There was never a party. Nobody came over. My mother would go to work as usual. On one occasion, when I was seventeen, she walked over to me with my present and card – yes, I did get those – and said:

'You do realize that if we'd had ultrasound scans in those days you wouldn't be standing here today.'

I don't know whether she was being deliberately provocative to see me react, or just wanted to hurt me. Maybe it was just a joke, I had no idea. It was a given in my life that anything could trigger off a verbal attack by my mother. Once, in my mid-twenties, I was over at Nessie's place, visiting. My mother and grandmother were there, too. I had been suffering from ovarian cysts and Nan asked me how I was doing. I replied that I didn't want to talk about it just then and I would call her on the phone the next day. She said fine and we carried on chatting about other things.

On the way home in the car my mother told me that I was never to speak to my grandmother in that way again and that I was to ring her the next day and apologize. What she was really doing was punishing me for a comment I made about Nessie. My mother thought Nessie was wonderful, and in many ways she was, but I was always compared to her and found wanting. Nessie's marriage and children were celebrated as if she had come home with an Olympic gold medal, but no matter what my achievements were – I was head girl at the school, won art competitions, was invited to join the Mouth and Foot Painters Association – she could never bring herself to acknowledge them. I can barely remember a single word of praise or encouragement from her during my entire childhood. At seventeen, I began to give up on our relationship. It was just too painful. I continued to see her from time to time throughout my twenties and thirties but my visits to Birmingham always left me battered and drained.

All my life I have longed for her love and approval but she could never bring herself to give it. The rest of the family never seemed to notice that our relationship was fraught in this way. That is what they claim, and it may be true to some extent, but I know how difficult it is to intervene where someone else's child is concerned. I think they preferred to turn a blind eye and not get involved. In any case, I don't know what they could have done to help. Our relationship is the way it is. Maybe it is her guilt. Maybe she just can't come to terms with the way I look. Maybe she resents my ambition and what she considers to be my southern English accent, which, in her view, is snobbish and superior. She thinks southerners are all pretentious and stuck up and that means me, too. I have acquired too many ideas above my station, which is true. I don't have the working-class Brummie upbringing of the rest of my family. And I have far greater expectations and ideas about what I want to achieve than my mother.

I don't think she has ever been able to come to terms with my disability and the fact that I'm not docile and quiet and happy to sit in a corner being unobtrusive. Just very recently I realized that she doesn't understand me or get where I'm coming from at all, and that realization has eased my angst considerably. And I've slowly come to acknowledge that I will never have the loving, accepting mother I've always wanted and she will never have the ordinary, fully limbed daughter that she'd wanted.

5

Lower Dorm

By the time I was five years old I had moved into the lower dorm, which was in another building. The nursing staff looked after us but it was auxiliary staff who supervised us. They were the disciplinarians and were almost military in their obsession with order and timekeeping, rigorously sticking to and maintaining the daily timetable of meals and tasks and events.

Lower dorm was a very difficult time because of the nature of the staff that they employed. I don't know anybody who has a good word to say about the period of time they spent there. And why is that? It's simple. They abused us. They exploited us. They terrorized us. There aren't any nicer words to describe it.

There was a particular little clique of staff whom I remember as being the ringleaders. They were the petty despots in our little province of lower dorm. I don't imagine they had a single qualification in looking after children between them. I have no idea why they were taken on. Maybe they were finding it difficult to find staff who would work there. The rates of pay were undoubtedly low. Or maybe they thought they would be able to keep discipline and order amongst us unruly kids. Whatever it was they were there and we were fair game and felt totally at their mercy. In those days there were no child protection agencies with laws and regulations and it seemed to us that nothing could keep them in check.

And it's a sickening thing to have to write but the children who were most impaired and the most vulnerable, much more so than me, were the ones they targeted for the worst abuses and mistreatment. The abuse was physical and emotional and although the physical was more dramatic and we were more shocked by that, it was the emotional battering that lasted longer. It left no visible scars, but I think many children were mentally scarred by their experiences.

I have to admit we were all cowards when it came to defending anyone who was suffering the attentions of those vicious bullies. When anything happened I was just glad that they hadn't picked on me. We lived our dormitory life in constant fear and anxiety. Of course, school was a safe haven during the week but only until four o'clock when our lessons finished. We all hung round in the classroom for as long as we could but eventually we would be pushed out to go back to the dorm and have our tea. The walk from the school back to lower dorm took about three minutes and every day we tried to make those three minutes last as long as possible. None of us wanted to get back too quickly or be the first in through the door because we never knew what to expect. We never knew who they were going to pick on or what they were going to do. I suppose that was another reason why we all liked school so much. The lessons might have been fun, dull or difficult but there was never any question of the teachers treating us like the staff back at lower dorm did.

There was one man who was very physically violent. And he was allowed to behave in any way that he wanted because there was nobody else around to stop him. He would often begin his entertainment by play fighting with one of us, usually one of the most impaired and weak of the children, and then just step over the line so that it wasn't play any more. What I mean by 'stepping over the line' is the point at which his slaps or kicks or punches started to hurt the child. Another of his favourite games was to pick us up and throw us across the room. It was a sort of tossing game with a bit of aiming and hitting the target thrown in. He would stand with one of us in his arms at one end of the playroom and then throw us in an arc across to the other side. I suppose the distance must have been fifteen or twenty feet. There were some cushions on the far side of the room that he aimed for and we were meant to land on them. Sometimes we did, but most of the time his aim missed the cushions altogether. When that happened we would hit the concrete and lino floor with a crack. If we hurt ourselves when we landed and found we were in pain, it was crucial not to cry out because he would then either shout at us or grab us and toss us even more violently towards the cushions.

It was extraordinary. Here was this untrained, unqualified man left alone in charge of a group of children, girls and boys, aged between five and eleven. But he wasn't the only one.

Unfortunately we couldn't trust the nurses to help us either because all the staff colluded with each other. It would be impossible for any nurse to defend one of us against one of her colleagues. On one occasion when the bullying had been particularly bad we decided to approach one of the teachers. We told her some of the things that had been happening in the dorm and asked whether she could help us to do something about it. She listened to everything we said and took it seriously enough to go to the head of nursing to tell her about it. I don't know exactly what was said in that meeting but the consequences for us children were typical. The sister in charge of our dorm told us off for telling lies to a teacher and we all received early bed punishments for a week. The teacher was reprimanded and told to keep her nose out of nursing affairs. And nothing changed.

The way we saw it was that we'd gone to an adult with our problems and she had done her best to try to help us, but it was all completely in vain and we suffered as a result. So we never tried getting help from a member of staff again. The situation was very simply adults against children. Them and us. It wasn't a question of our word against theirs. That didn't come into it. For the staff we were automatically always in the wrong in any argument between staff and children because everything we did, as far as they were concerned, was either us trying to cause trouble or us trying to get attention.

Of course, not all the staff at the children's home were pure sadists. Some were wonderful and very caring. But many of the younger ones and the unqualified ones didn't give a stuff about us. They seemed to enjoy being cruel. Most of it was very petty but their aggressive teasing and ridiculing took place day in and day out. It made dorm life very miserable most of the time. There was one particular member of staff, a man, who didn't like me. I don't know why he didn't like me, he just didn't – and I didn't like him.

I was a very poor eater back then. The staff had their own theories as to why but as far I was concerned it was simple: the cooked food was disgusting – tasteless vegetables that had been boiled for hours and the cheapest pies they could find. Anyway, on this particular morning I was looking out of the dorm window and saw a delivery lorry drive in through the gates and back up into the area behind the kitchens. It was loaded with fresh fruit, enough for the entire site for the whole week, so we are talking a big lorry and a lot of fruit. I always looked forward to the arrival of the fruit lorry because it was such a pleasure to eat something that tasted good instead of the usual overcooked stodge. I waited until lunchtime and then during the meal I asked this particular member of staff if I could have an orange after I had finished eating.

'No, you can't.'

'Why not?'

'Because there aren't any oranges.'

'But I saw the fruit lorry arrive this morning.'

'No, you didn't. And don't argue with me or you'll never get any fruit again. What you actually saw, Miss Clever-clever, was the laundry supplies van. And funnily enough the laundry van doesn't deliver fruit.'

I knew what was going on. He didn't like me and he didn't want me to have an orange, so he simply lied. Well, I wasn't going to let it go, so I waited a few minutes until he left the dining room for a moment and then asked another member of staff instead. She was happy enough to get one and peel it for me and I set about enjoying every delicious mouthful. I love fresh fruit.

Later it turned out that she was a pal of his, something I was blissfully unaware of at the time. I was chomping away on my juicy orange, when he suddenly appeared. 'Where did you get that orange from?' In my innocent voice I said, 'Oh, *she* gave it to me', nodding in the woman's direction. I admit I was slightly gloating, but I also felt totally justified in my actions. I thought I was perfectly entitled to have an orange and in a way I felt I was doubly entitled because he had lied to me. After all, we were being brought up not to lie, to always tell the truth, and yet this man felt that he could lie to me whenever it suited him. Even though I was only a young girl, I knew he was being petty and unfair, and that it was wrong of him to behave like that. But he had the power.

This man went to find the woman who had given me the orange and between them they concluded that I had done something wrong and would have to be dealt with. I was in the dining room with about fifty other kids when he came storming back and stood in front of me. I turned in my seat and waited for what he had to say. He was livid with anger and got straight into it. In front of all the other children he shouted, his face about six inches from mine.

'You're too big for your boots, you are, Alison Lapper. I said you couldn't have an orange so you bloody well went behind my back, didn't you. You're an . . . an . . . ungrateful spoiled little madam.'

There was quite a lot more in that vein and I sat still listening for several minutes. He was loud and intense, and not holding back his feelings at all because he was so angry. I slowly went white and shrank into my seat. I was shocked. I hadn't thought for a second that my cheeky idea to ask someone else for the orange would end like that.

The punishment they decided would be appropriate for me was ridiculously excessive given what I'd done, and for as long as it lasted it made my life totally miserable. They made sure that every night I was in bed by six o'clock. That meant that I would get back from school at around 4.15 in the afternoon. I would have time for tea, but not supper, and then I was sent to bed. This was in the middle of summer, when it was still broad daylight and all my friends were still up and about, playing and doing things together. In the meantime, I was forced to lie in my bed listening to them chatting and larking around on the grass outside while I stared at the ceiling. This was my punishment for defying authority and asking for an orange. And they made absolutely sure that I stuck to the punishment.

On one occasion I was late making the six o'clock curfew because I had to wait my turn for a bath and the auxiliary who was in charge of bathing that evening had told me to go and wait in the playroom; she would come and call me when it was my turn. Naturally this member of staff was doing his rounds at just that time and spotted me in there playing with my friends. 'Alison Lapper, why aren't you in bed?' he screamed across the room. I tried to explain to him that I was waiting my turn to have a bath and that the auxiliary had told me to stay in the playroom until I was called. He refused to listen and just dragged me off to my bed. In those days, staff were able to deal with us very physically, just pick us up and put us here or pull us there. There were very few constraints. Everyone just turned a blind eye and if any of us complained to someone higher up we were never believed or marked down as troublemakers, usually both.

As I lay in my bed after he left I got really upset. I tried to grit my teeth and be hard. I hated letting them get to me but we were all so close to the edge emotionally that the slightest thing could set us off. I couldn't stop crying and what angered me the most was that there was no question of the bathing auxiliary speaking up for me and telling him that what I had said was true and it wasn't my fault. No chance. Many of the staff were in cahoots with each other, colluding in everyday injustices like the bathtime incident. And there was no point in talking to one of the more caring staff because that would have caused even more trouble for me from the likes of this person. He had total authority and power over me and enjoyed exercising it whenever he had the chance.

Fortunately, not all members of staff were like him. Some of the other people who looked after me treated me as a worthwhile individual, or at least acknowledged that I had a personality that was all my own. I was befriended by a really kind physiotherapist, Margaret, and she sometimes took a particular group of us for little outings. It was a group made up of those children whose parents never came down on open days, and who never went home for weekends. Margaret would take us to her house, or to her friend's house, and they would cook a slap-up roast lunch. We would have a great day away from our dorms in a different, humane world and loved every minute of it. But even the kind efforts of staff like Margaret were often negated by those whose main purpose in life seemed to be making things as unpleasant as possible.

At that time I was always made to wear dresses that were too short for me. I was conscious from a very early age that my knickers were always showing but there was nothing I could do. I had no money to buy anything so I had to wear what I was given.

Margaret was well aware of my clothes situation and on one of the outings to have lunch at her house she took me clothes shopping. We went from shop to shop looking at clothes in all the different styles. Eventually something caught my eye and I tried it on in the customers' changing room. It fitted perfectly and when I asked Margaret if I could have it, she said yes. It was the first thing I had ever chosen for myself, a very seventies dress – psychedelic with its oranges and yellows. I was really thrilled about it. I got back to the dorm after our day out and, of course, I had my new dress on. I was so proud of it. I felt comfortable and, for once, I was wearing a dress that covered my bottom. And I couldn't stop smiling. Of course, my least favourite staff member was ready and waiting.

'Where did you get that?'

'Margaret bought it for me.'

'I bet you asked her for it, didn't you? You made her buy it. She goes to all that trouble taking you out and you con her into buying clothes for Little Miss High and Mighty Lapper. You devious little cow!'

He carried on ranting about how I didn't deserve anything, let alone a new dress. Then made me take the dress off. I had to change into some other clothes for the evening. My new dress was confiscated and I didn't get it back until it was too small for me. All the staff knew what he'd done but everyone kept quiet. I still don't understand why he had such a problem with me and why he had to behave so badly. Years later I told Margaret about it and she wanted to know why I hadn't said anything to her. I explained that if I had told her at the time the consequences for me would have been even worse than just losing the dress. It wasn't worth it, so I kept quiet. If you are frightened, you keep quiet. I missed that dress. It was the first one that I'd ever been allowed to choose and buy, but just as bad was the feeling that he left me with: that I didn't deserve nice things.

In addition to the nurses and wardens, the home had a full complement of teachers who taught us the same subjects you would find in any school. They were fully qualified professionals and almost all of them were fully committed to teaching us as best they could. There was no bullying, taunting or mocking by any of the teachers in the school. Because of that the school side of the home became a kind of haven for all the children. Although we were still confined to the site it was still a chance for me to have a respite from the regular maulings in lower dorm. In my mid-twenties I was finally diagnosed as having dyslexia but this had never been spotted before. The general view among the teaching staff was that as far as academic work was concerned I was just a bit stupid. Even so, I found many of the lessons interesting and sometimes even inspiring. I always looked forward to going to school.

There was a wonderful English teacher called Jane Barton. She lived in a converted stable with her cats and would tell us endless stories about them and her home. I would listen spellbound to what were probably very everyday tales of her life. But we were all fascinated by what went on in the outside world, how people lived, what their homes looked like, where they went. Miss Barton's openness was unusual. There were very few adults who took the time to tell us about themselves, to talk to us about their lives, their families and their pets. People didn't talk to us like that normally. But she did.

For some reason we were never taught table manners at the children's home and Miss Barton took it upon herself to tackle this. She didn't have to, it wasn't part of her job description, but for some reason of her own she was very keen that we should learn how to behave in a civilized manner. Once a week she would come to the lower dorm side and we would have a little tea party. We all sat around in a neat little circle and ate sugar and golden syrup sandwiches. They were not nutritionally the best thing for us but I remember them as being the most delicious sandwiches I have ever eaten. When we ate with her during these little tea parties we abandoned our usual style of grabbing food and wolfing it down and throwing it about. Instead, we ate more slowly, with our mouths closed, and said things to each other like: 'After you' and 'Could you please pass the biscuits, thank you'. We poured each other cups of tea into white china cups. If you knew how we usually behaved when we ate our meals you would have been amazed at the transformation, but we really enjoyed behaving 'proper' because of Miss Barton.

And because this all happened outside school hours, Jane asked us to call her by her nickname which was Bartbox. So Bartbox she became whenever she came in to have one of her little tea parties. I loved calling her that because it made our relationship more informal and more intimate. But, once again, the staff in the dormitory started having their feathers ruffled by our friendship with Jane Barton. One of the sisters heard me referring to Jane as Bartbox and pulled me into her office for a chat. She told me that I must stop calling Miss Barton Bartbox and that if she heard me use that nickname again I would be punished. Why? Was she jealous of our friendly relationship? Were we enjoying ourselves too much? What the hell was it that drove them to stamp on every little relaxation and easing of our situation. The next day she talked to the whole of the dorm. We were given a lecture about manners and told that the teas would be allowed to continue but we had to call Bartbox 'Miss Barton'. At the next tea party we all asked Miss Barton if it was still okay to call her Bartbox. We thought she would say: 'Yes, of course you can.' But Sister had already talked to her about it and she was forced to inform us that Sister wanted us to stop calling her Bartbox because it was disrespectful. The stupid thing was that I was never disrespectful to Jane, none of us were, because we liked her and because she always treated us with respect as well.

I loved being in Jane Barton's English classes even though I wasn't a particularly good student because of my dyslexia. She never made me feel stupid and was very patient with my slow and laboured reading and writing. Last thing on a Friday afternoon, when we had finished our lessons, Jane would let me sit up on a wooden draining board next to a row of stainless steel sinks which ran along the side of the classroom. It was a nice place for me because the wood was warm to sit on. I can remember it so clearly. Jane would give me all the paint pots that needed washing out and I would play with water and paint and all the messy used paint pots. It was my favourite thing to do because I loved mixing the colours and playing with them, making them run in ever-changing patterns in the sinks. I would do that for hours, or for as long as I was allowed to.

Every single child at the home had one thing in common: we all loved to get out of the institution and into the world outside where everybody else lived. We were fascinated by it, attracted to it and yearned for it every day. And we looked forward with desperate anticipation to any little outing that took us beyond the gates. Each school class had at least one outing a term and these trips could range from the most enthralling, like a trip to London Zoo, to the more mundane, like a trip to the waterworks.

We had been visiting the local prison since I was three. I don't know why they chose a prison for us to visit. Maybe it was meant to show the prisoners that there were other people worse off than themselves, people who had no choice in the matter. Perhaps, then, they would feel less unfortunate themselves and possibly, somehow, regret their antisocial habits and turn over a new leaf. Maybe the fact that it was close to the home was the reason. In any case it didn't matter to us. It was just another opportunity for an exciting day out.

We were driven into the prison in our blue minibus and the guards checked to see that we weren't smuggling in any forbidden items. They knew who we were and why we were coming, but they went through the motions anyway. Then the tall prison gates were shut behind us and the driver parked our minibus in the forecourt. We all sat inside, waiting and wondering. After a short while a squad of male prisoners wearing their blue prison overalls boarded the bus. We looked at them and they looked at us and neither group knew what to think. The nurse who was in charge of us made some kind of introduction, while we waited patiently to see what would happen. The prisoners must have already been told what they had to do. They came to our seats, undid our seatbelts and picked us up. Then, one by one, each with a child tucked under his arm, they got off the bus and walked back inside the prison buildings.

Still tucked safely under the prisoners' arms we found ourselves passing big recreational rooms and communal bathrooms and dining rooms. Everything was drab and plain, with paint peeling off the walls. I recognized the familiar white and pale green walls and the grubby formica surfaces. It looked so familiar, very much like the place I lived in, and for a time I honestly thought the home was just another prison. But during the course of the day I worked out that the men were in there because they were being punished for bad things that they had done. It didn't matter to me, though, because they were so nice to us. When I asked two of them what they'd done to get themselves sent to prison, one said he was in for robbery and the other for fraud. I had no idea what fraud was but I nodded my head anyway. The prison didn't have any rapists or murderers. Or if there were they didn't let on.

My prisoner, the one who carried me in, was a tall, muscular black man called Charlie, who was very sweet to me all day. I thought he was extremely handsome and charming and he told me he thought I was cute. We were quite a pair. All that day he scarcely put me down once and everywhere he went I went.

At one point he took me into one of the recreation rooms which we hadn't been in before. It was a big room with a high ceiling like a school gymnasium and in the centre they had built a Red Indian tepee as a present for us kids. What a sight it was, although it looked rather out of place in its plain surroundings. It was huge and colourful, and towered up above me towards the ceiling. All around its base they had painted buffaloes and a hunting party of Red Indians on horses chasing after them and firing arrows. I walked around it slowly so that I could see all the things that had been so accurately painted. Someone at the prison must have been a very good artist before he began his life of crime.

When we had been around it a couple of times, Charlie asked me if I wanted to look inside. I wasn't sure. I did and I didn't. Charlie was teasing me by being very mysterious about it. I could see a flap which had been pulled across to reveal the inside. The hole was big enough for us to enter but it was dark inside and I suddenly felt nervous about going in, although I was also very curious.

'What's inside there, Charlie? Tell me. I'll go inside if you tell me.' But he wouldn't.

In the end I plucked up the courage and he carried me into the dark interior. It was totally empty – except for one thing, a looming life-sized figure of a witch complete with warts and mouldy rotten teeth. 'Get me *out* of here!' I screamed. It was the scariest thing I'd ever seen.

After that he took me to see his cell, which wasn't officially allowed but he did anyway. There wasn't much in it, but I was thrilled to be in there because it was against the rules. It really was exciting visiting a prison. Charlie and I joined up with the rest of the prisoners and children for lunch in a big refectory. The food was very similar to what we ate, except the portions were much larger. The catering staff in the prison didn't seem to be able to tell the difference between a 5-year-old's appetite and that of a grown man. I picked at my food as usual and didn't eat much.

When lunch was over we all went back to the recreation

room. Charlie took me in and put me down and I sat there wide-eyed. The big teepee had disappeared and an elaborate and beautifully painted roundabout was there in its place. The prisoners had been working on it for months and all we kids thought it was wonderful. Later that week, it was brought over to the children's home and some of the prisoners put it together for us in the grounds. It had cute little seats, two by two, instead of the usual fairground horses, which we would have fallen off.

Far too soon for my liking the day came to an end and it was time for us to go back. The same squad of prisoners picked up the children they had been assigned to for the day and we all walked in single file out to the prison car park. Both Charlie and I were feeling sad. We had both had a great time together but the minibus was waiting with our driver and the guards had already opened the big prison gates ready for us to leave.

Charlie and his mate, Ron, were putting me back on the bus and both looked over at the open gates. I heard Charlie say, 'Shall we make a run for it, Ronnie?' I looked up in alarm. Was I going to be part of a prison breakout? Ron replied, 'We'd better not Charlie. We're going to be out in two weeks.' They were having a little joke and I laughed along with them. The visits to the prison held very happy memories. I never felt scared or apprehensive. It was just somewhere to go where we had fun.

Every Wednesday we had visitors to the school. I remember the well-meaning folk from outside who came to see us. I was always fascinated by these people – their look and just the fact of them being there. They were more new faces from the out-side world. It wasn't that far removed from those Hollywood films where some well-heeled and glamorous couple goes to the local dog pound to adopt a stray puppy. The camera shows the audience all the different puppies one by one in their little cages, all wide-eyed and eager to be the one leaving with their new owner. The two Hollywood stars walk slowly along look-ing at each dog until they eventually stop at one of the cages. They look at each other, smiling and nodding, and pick up a cute little puppy dog which they stroke and cuddle. The scene ends with them leaving with their new pet that they put gently into the back of their limo-sized car with the leather seats. 'Let's call it Scruffy, darling!'

These visitors were a regular occurrence. They would be shown round the site in a group and would peer through the windows of our classrooms. Very often they would be brought inside for a closer look as well. They were not our parents or anyone that knew us personally. Basically, they were the people who gave money to the home. They had come to have a look at us and to see what their money was being spent on. And they had the look of money. They were nicely dressed, in that middle-class sort of way: smart coats and a certain smell that I always imagined people with money smelled of – lavender and leather.

And I remember the looks on their faces: horror and pity. They seemed to be thinking: Oh my God! This is horrific. What on earth am I looking at? They didn't understand at all what they were seeing. We were just an ordinary group of young human beings who happened to have missing limbs and twisted bodies. What they saw was a gaggle of pitiful monsters. I can see them now, all huddled together close to the door and looking as if they'd just entered a hospital ward for incurable infectious diseases.

Am I being too hard on them? Probably. They were prime examples of the admirable but forlorn charitable urge of the English middle classes. I think in fairness they were very happy to be parting with their money for our benefit, but I really don't think they had any idea who we were at all. For our part we thoroughly enjoyed their presence in our classroom. We had all been playing to the gallery in one form or another for many years. I'm sure that we intuitively understood the subtleties of the situation and, probably without realizing it, performed like circus clowns for the visitors with their money and their charitable urges. We clicked our hydraulic arms and showed them our stumps and walked our funny walks for them. We certainly weren't inhibited or embarrassed, and we liked having them there.

I may have had a reputation for being gregarious, loud and cheeky but I know I also spent a lot of time on my own, in my own little world. From an early age I was a solitary figure but I think a lot of people would not recognize that side of me. I did a lot of things just by myself, retreating into my own little world of the imagination. I loved playing with my doll collection. I call it a collection but it was probably only five or six dolls, Barbies and Sindys, which had been given to me over the years as Christmas presents by my family. Even when I was older, perhaps thirteen or fourteen, I was still playing with them. On a Saturday or Sunday, when we had free time,

I would go up to the dormitory and I would get my dolls out of my locker. Then I would lay them all out in a row and dress them in the tiny clothes I thought they should be wearing on that day. When I was satisfied with how they looked I would sit there, on the floor between the beds, and play with them all day. Sometimes my best friend, Tara, would play with me too but if she got fed up with it I would still carry on playing by myself.

I made up little romantic stories in which the dolls represented various characters. I think I had one Action Man doll to take on any male roles. Actually, the stories I made up were more like tragedies. The girls were always hungry and cold, or brokenhearted, or trying to escape from some unknown dreadful thing. I think I finally managed to pack them away for good when I was fifteen.

When my interest in dolls finally faded, I replaced my escapes into the world of dolly tragedies with hours and hours spent in front of the television. I had my own special chair for viewing programmes. And when I wasn't watching television, I was drawing. I drew stick people and invented the same tragic stories for them. The women would get pregnant, always out of wedlock, and their men would walk out on them, never to be seen again. It was always hard times for my poor stick characters.

In my last two years in lower dorm, the strangest thing happened. Many of the staff began to treat us like human beings. Some even invited us to their homes or took us on outings. I can't explain why it happened but I remember it clearly.

————

6

Upper Dorm

At the age of eleven I moved up to the senior section at the children's home – upper dorm. The building consisted of a long corridor with annexes leading off on either side, ideal for dormitories. The girls slept upstairs and the boys slept downstairs, and once again Tara and I had beds next to each other. We were a good bunch of girls all piled in together and most of the time got on pretty well.

At the beginning, upper dorm was not dissimilar to lower dorm. Each dormitory had a head warden and then more wardens who worked under them, just like the lower dorm. But by the time I had arrived at the age of eleven it wasn't possible to be terrorized on quite the same scale. I was getting physically bigger and stronger and mentally much tougher, and I was more able to stand up for myself.

Soon the oppressive system of heavy-handed discipline administered by unqualified staff came to an end. I suppose rumours of untoward activities must have drifted up to the higher levels of authority at the home. They put an end to the old system and the head wardens were aided by a house mother for each dorm. They wanted to make it a more family-like atmosphere. The house mother whom I had really did want to mother us all, but by then none of us wanted that. We had grown too independent and had established our own self-generated way of coping and surviving. These days, the children's home is a friendly place and the children are very well cared for. However, for us it was too little too late.

We had been there for more than ten years and were developing the mental capacity to analyse how we had been treated and what was happening to us. And in spite of all the kindnesses and well-meaning efforts by the staff on our behalf, it was still them versus us. By then I was viewing them as a group of able-bodied, middle-class adults who were there to control us and change us and fix us up to be as much like them as possible. They saw us only from their perspective and there wasn't much that any of us could do to change that point of view. Ultimately, it didn't matter whether they were kind or cruel, lax or stern, in the final analysis we couldn't trust them because they saw us in such a fixed way.

There was a distinction between the people who were custodial staff, like the wardens, and professional medical staff.

Janet Darby was the radiographer during my time there. She took all the photographs of me and was typical of the best professionals who worked there. I liked her. She was a type: middle class, correct, professional and kind, but I always felt that she never questioned the ethos of the place, the underlying values and principles which guided the institution and allowed the children to be dealt with like pawns. Maybe that sounds harsh but I don't mean it to be. I always looked forward to my sessions with Janet. She wore a green laboratory coat and always had her dog with her. I would talk to her in my mildly cheeky style while I stroked her dog. Animals were a novelty for us and we were all drawn to other people's pets when they showed up in our world. It was also true that on these occasions I had Janet all to myself and as it was rare for any of us to have the exclusive attention of an adult for more than a brief moment in the day, I treasured the time that I spent with her.

Each session was informal and light. When I asked her whether I could watch her developing the results of our session, she always said yes. It was exciting and I appreciated being allowed to accompany her inside her darkroom. I would sit on a high stool, bathed in orange light, and watch the photographs magically appear on the paper as she tilted them back and forth in their chemical bath. She took both X-rays and photographs and when I sat and watched her at work I felt a part of something real.

But as with everything else at the home the photography had its other side. When I was young I didn't really understand the context of the photographs being taken. They were a sort of medical record and our co-oporation was always assumed, as with everything else the school told us to do. When I got older I became more uncomfortable with the photographs that were taken of me. Sometimes it wasn't possible to take the photographs in Janet's laboratory for some reason, so she would come over to the main building and take pictures of me in some spare room like the dining room. But it wasn't private. I would be stripped down to my bra and panties and people would be walking past through the swing doors on their way from one part of the building to another. She was very bright and breezy about it as if it didn't matter and because I had such a good relationship with her I didn't want to spoil it by creating a fuss.

I want to be fair to Janet. I am sure she was not conscious of doing anything that might affect us adversely. She was just doing her job in the way that it had always been done, in the way that was thought best. It is only now that I can look back and see what happened to me from a different perspective, and I'm not seeking to blame anyone for anything. Susannah Child told me recently that she thought the home was the making of me. And although I hate to agree with her unreservedly, there is some truth in what she said.

On another occasion, the home had invited or hired a film crew to make a film about us – a kind of day in the life. The finished film was kept and shown to doctors and others. In one scene I was shown being lifted out of bed by one of the dormitory staff. The reality was that no one ever lifted me out of my bed at that age. I always had to do it for myself. It was a soapy, soft focus version of things designed to be shown to people who might be encouraged to give money to the institution. Of course, those of us who were chosen were all thrilled to be in the film, which was produced with a real director and film crew. They were able to use us in the film, so freely because some of us, Tara and me included, had permission from our parents to be photographed. There were many children who did not. For three days, I did nothing but appear in different scenes for the film. I was eleven years old and I loved it.

When I was twelve, we had a male carer called Chris, who later became a vicar. He was good at his job and we all liked having him in charge of us, but we were also becoming teenage girls. Our breasts were developing and we all had regular periods. Chris still bathed us and toileted us and we were beginning to get a little bit uncomfortable with that. I don't think that could happen today. We were told that if we wanted to keep him in charge of us then we would have to continue to allow him to bathe us and take us to the toilet. It was a difficult choice because we all liked him and wanted him to stay. In the end we reluctantly accepted that we would have to let him deal with our personal care.

Chris was a big beefy man, well over six feet tall and extremely strong. One summer Sunday evening, we were sitting and chatting and getting bored. I don't know who had the idea but all twelve of us agreed that it was a good one. One of us went into the bathroom and ran a full bath of cold water. Then I called Chris, who was sitting reading the Sunday paper, saying one of the girls was having problems in the bath.

We stripped him down to his underpants and were all trying hard to get them off as we bundled him into the bath and the waiting cold water. I think we had squeezed all our toothpaste tubes and other liquid toiletries into the bath as well. The noise of our shrieking and screaming was deafening and could probably be heard all over the building. But we didn't care. We were in a frenzy, like something out of *Lord of the Flies*. It must have been a crazy sight: Chris all but naked in the bath and us girls all around him squeezing toothpaste on his hair and body. We were at the height of our fun when the deputy head warden arrived.

'WHAT is going on?' he shouted at the top of his voice.

We all turned to face him and fell silent in an instant.

He was furious with us and with Chris, who sheepishly emerged from the bath clutching his sodden underpants. We were punished with early bedtimes and the loss of some privileges for a few weeks but it didn't make any difference. Most of the time we were well-behaved and cooperative, but when we went crazy, we went crazy.

We were always playing pranks on Chris. Maybe that's why we liked him so much. On another occasion he took us swimming at the pool. As we splashed round in the water, one by one each girl got out of the pool and sneaked into the changing room. And one by one each returned with all the separate articles from his pile of clothes and dived back into the pool. It was like a comedy display from a swimming gala. One girl, I think it was Tara, did a balletic dive with Chris's flat cap on her head. He loved that cap, but it was ruined once she submerged it in the water. Someone else took his socks and tied them on to the chrome step rail at the bottom of the deep end. All the while he kept saying, 'Now, now, girls. That's enough. You've had your fun.' But we didn't stop. It took him a long time to gather all the items and all the while we were shrieking with laughter and saying things like: 'Have you seen your socks lately, Chris?' He had to dress himself in sopping wet clothes and take us back to the dormitory dripping with water.

If I'm honest I have to say that we were always ready to play a prank on just about anybody who came our way, whether they were staff or not. One Saturday morning we had some visitors to our dorm. They were the parents of girls in upper dorm and one particular couple seemed to us especially toffee-nosed. We had the impression they looked down on us as if we weren't good enough to be companions to their daughter. Of course, we couldn't attack them directly in any way. Instead, we put one of our pet hamsters down the back of one of the young care staff. The effect was dramatic. The little creature was squirming about inside her top and she couldn't get at it with her hands to pull it out. She rushed about screaming: 'Get it out! Get it out!' We just laughed and watched her twist her body in all directions trying to dislodge the little pet. The snooty parents, who were sitting on their daughter's bed, seemed unable to believe what they were seeing. They went straight to our house leader and reported the incident. They described what had happened and complained that we were unruly and rude, and that we treated the staff abominably. Once again we got into big trouble.

Then there were the water fights. These were a spectacular summer activity that came about spontaneously. All they required was a warm night and the children hanging about full of pent-up energy and nothing to expend it on. One minute we would all be sitting around outside chatting and the next everyone would have a cup or a jug or some other receptacle in their mouth or hands or feet, and everyone would be chucking water at everyone else. Sometimes the jug would follow on with the water and we would have to duck to avoid being hit.

Soon the next dormitory would be doing the same thing, and the next, until the boys downstairs were also joining in. Before long, all 100 children were having an extended water fight all over the upper dorm building and because there were so many of us it was almost impossible for the staff to stop what we were doing. In fact, they often joined in. I'm sure they were as bored and pent up with the institutional routines as we were.

Water attacks and counterattacks would continue for up to two hours and by the end of that time both the upper and lower floors of the building were swimming in inches of water. It was more like a water riot than a water fight, and the water was not confined to the floors. There was water trickling down the lift shaft and running down the stairs in a stream. We ignored the danger and groups of girls would cram into the lift armed with full water jugs and invade the boys' territory on the floor below. We must have been extremely lucky not to electrocute ourselves.

All our water riots ended in the same way. The deputy

head warden would return from his evening out, hear of it and go purple with anger at the chaos. He would race round the building going from dorm to dorm and floor to floor.

'Stop this fighting right now! You're behaving like a bunch of animals! What the hell do you think you're playing at! Put those jugs down at once!'

And then we'd have to clear everything up. The staff would also receive a dressing down but that was never done in the presence of the children. I know they always claimed that there was nothing they could do because there were too many of us, which was true.

We had water fights about two or three times during the summer. The heat and the confinement, our mundane institutional life, would build up a tension in all of us and at a certain point we would lose it, lose control. The girls were more prone to letting off steam in this way because of their periods.

The group of twelve girls that I was part of menstruated at exactly the same time and when we were premenstrual together anything could happen. It was a new development for us but soon became a major factor in our moods, in our lives and in our conversation. We frequently discussed it amongst ourselves but we didn't call it a 'period' or use the word 'menstruate'. We said: 'Aunt Jane is coming to stay'. I don't know who invented that phrase but it was probably a staff member who found calling a spade a spade distasteful. The staff were from the generation which liked to say 'I'm going to powder my nose' instead of 'I'm going to the toilet.'

We loved copying the euphemisms used by grown-ups

and the one which substituted for the word period was a favourite. When Aunt Jane arrived we were tense and catty with each other and in her wake fights or arguments would break out continuously. The female staff who lived on site were also in sync with the girls. So they would also be catty and tense, too. Our worst behaviour was always reserved for full moons or when we had our periods and when the two coincided some sort of riot was certain.

By a bizarre coincidence they always seemed to serve a cherry cheesecake at lunch on the day that we got our periods. The white cheese was laced with threads of red which naturally reminded us of menstrual blood. We would make all kinds of remarks about Aunt Jane's arrival and try to outdo each other with ever more disgusting words. One of the wardens, a married middle-aged man, had stood himself near the lunch table so that he could hear our conversation. We were serving up the cheesecake and saying things like: 'Ooh, what does this remind you of?' and 'Has anyone seen Aunt Jane's car parked outside?' It wasn't any of his business and shouldn't have been a conversation of interest to him. After listening to us talk for a considerable time he reported us to our house leader for filthy talk, adding a load of sanctimonious twaddle about how 'disturbed' he was. How can any man have real insight into what it means for a young girl to have periods and what importance might lie in the chatter of young girls when they come on. But the house leader agreed with him and we received yet another reprimand. We were a group of young girls experiencing our first periods and trying to make sense of the extraordinary things that were happening to our bodies.

And as far as that aspect of our lives was concerned, he didn't have a clue.

Dorm life was monotonous and repetitive. I lived, like all the other children, under a cloud of anxiety, fear and longing. But there were still times of the year when life in the dorm, by some miracle, became wondrous and magical.

Christmas was one of those special times. Everyone suddenly became much more light-hearted and cheerful: the kids, the people who drove the buses and the people who got you up in the morning, teachers, nurses even wardens, everybody. It was a time when I can honestly say I loved being there. I always enjoyed Christmastime from as far back as I can remember right up until the time I left the children's home at seventeen. The magic of it never left me even when I reached the age when I knew Father Christmas no longer existed.

I was in a dormitory with about fifteen other girls and we were having our morning inspection. At Christmas, the strict morning inspections were transformed into a completely different kind of occasion. The room was laid out in cubicles, so there would be three or sometimes four beds and then a partition. The partitions were really just screens, they didn't reach as far as the floor or as high as the ceiling. Bed and a locker, bed and a locker, bed and a locker, screen, and so on. At that time many of us had little musical jewellery boxes that were all the rage. Of course, we didn't have any jewels, just the boxes.

Anita and Janice, a couple of the staff members, who still had a bit of fun left in them, gathered up all our jewellery boxes and wound them up. Then they opened the lids and left them hidden in cupboards, drawers, under beds, all over the place. We could hear their little tinkling tunes coming from all four corners of the dorm, high and low.

A couple of minutes later the head female warden breezed in to make sure everything was neat and ready. She stopped in her tracks and heard the sounds of all those jewellery boxes coming from everywhere. Her face had a wonderful look of panic because she could hear them but couldn't see them. She rushed round like a lunatic trying to find all the boxes to shut them up before the head male warden came round to do the inspection. We were all splitting our sides laughing. We were free to enjoy ourselves in that way because it wasn't us who had hidden the boxes and because it was Christmas. Of course, we knew where the jewellery boxes had been hidden but we weren't going to say anything. And she couldn't find them because there wasn't enough time and here was the deputy head warden coming in through the door. So the inspection began and the jewellery boxes were still all playing away. We loved it and couldn't stop giggling. The whole inspection had this sense of fun about it, which even the wardens seemed to share.

In the evening Anita and Janice put us all to bed, ready for lights out. We were all lying there cosy and snug in our beds, when the two of them all of a sudden started lobbing toilet rolls over the dividing partitions. We immediately joined in using our dressing sticks or crutches and tossed them back. Straightaway another loo roll came flying over the screen unravelling as it went. Back and forth the loo rolls went, all of us screeching and laughing until we were inches deep in a huge mess of toilet paper. It would be unthinkable for us to behave like that normally but because the staff were doing it with us it was allowed. None of us had any idea why we were being allowed to make such an incredible mess. If we had done it by ourselves we would have been in big trouble. Things like that always seemed to happen around Christmas time.

The most magical part of all this celebration and gaiety for me was that the dormitories would get decorated. Each year every dormitory would have a theme. I remember one year our dormitory did Snow White and the seven dwarfs. I don't know who did all the artwork but it was brilliantly well done. Every dwarf was meticulously cut out and painted and the whole dormitory became like a stage set. There wasn't a square inch of the room which wasn't decorated. The fairy lights were strung from wall to wall in long looping arcs. It was beautiful. Enchanting. Even our beds had cardboard painted figures stuck on to the headboards. It was like walking into our very own Christmas grotto.

In my early years at the home I wasn't aware of being different because everyone around me was also. I could see that some of us were able to run round more easily because they had good use of their legs and others needed wheelchairs, but I simply accepted that as fact. It wasn't until the age of twelve, when I became more self-aware, that I began to notice people's reactions. I mean the reactions of able-bodied people in the world outside. And that's when it really began to hit me. I was a teenager, desperate to be part of the outside world, but I was beginning to realize it could never happen because that world didn't want me to be part of it. I was never going to be the same as the non-disabled children of my own age because there was a huge barrier between us. And they could not get past it to make me part of their group. However much I overcompensated to try to join them, I never could break through. I followed the same bands that other girls were following. I dressed in the same clothes that I saw them wearing and used the same make-up, but none of it made any difference.

It didn't stop me from trying though. I suppose that's what being desperate means. The local youth club had a disco on Thursdays and every other week a group of the older kids was allowed to attend the club. Our arrival in our special transport set the scene. The special kids from the special school were arriving.

Tara and I and the others in our group walked into the first room, where we signed the register at a table just inside the door. The bar had sweets and drinks that we could buy and, of course, we did. We wanted to do what everyone else did, to look as normal as possible. A second room held the disco and that was what we had come for. Tara and I both loved music and dancing. We watched *Top of the Pops* every week and avidly followed the charts and the latest bands. Once we had gone through to the second room we clung together as a group at one end and the able-bodied kids were at the other. We wanted to mingle, to chat and hang out with the group at the other end, but we didn't know how to do it. Maybe they were as keen to talk to us as we were to talk to them. It was just them in their group and us in ours. There was almost no intermingling.

We still loved being there because it was a night out and there was loud music and we could dance. When we weren't dancing, Tara and I stayed close to our wall looking out for good-looking boys and talking about them and putting on our lip gloss every five minutes. 'Is he? Is he looking at me? Yes, I think he is.' 'Don't look now, he'll see us looking.'

We drank our lemonade with carefree panache, pretending it was alcohol, and enjoyed every minute. It was typical teenage life but it was rationed. Just once every other Thursday. We didn't have nearly enough exposure to other teenagers and they didn't have enough exposure to us. So they never got to know us and relationships didn't develop. We always had to leave early, whereas they could stay till the end of the disco and, perhaps, go on to someone else's house and keep the party going. We on the other hand would be heading off down the road in the special bus back to the special school. The journey home was full of laughter and telling stories about the night. Even though we knew it was another them-and-us situation, yet again we accepted it. We believed that was the way it was for people like us.

In many respects the regime in upper dorm had changed for the better. I had a locker by my bed and I was allowed to keep certain things and possess them as my own. They had dispensed with the chests they had in lower dorm where everything was communal property and none of us could own anything, even if it was a Christmas present given to us by our parents.

Another improvement was the fact that I was allowed to give up my artificial arms, which had never worked for me.

Other children had also been allowed to give up limbs which caused them difficulty. So mealtimes were less comical than before. Well, that's not entirely accurate. Whereas meals in lower dorm had been unintentionally comical because we had so little control over our prostheses, now the comedy was more a result of our intentional acts. All of us were much more adept at using what parts of limbs we had and the meal table was an excellent arena for us to practise our ever-improving motor abilities.

By the age of thirteen I was getting heavier and, as my body developed, my feet were becoming more and more swollen and painful. My right ankle bone, if you can imagine it, was the size of a golf ball, and my heel was in the air. So the whole of the right side of my right foot was on the floor. And the heel and the toes, which should have been on the floor, were all in the air. My weight was bearing entirely on a single bone and it hurt constantly. Of course, I was used to having pain in my life. I was missing bits and my body structure wasn't correct enough to take all the stresses of moving about. So pain was a constant, always there in the background. But this new pain was different and close to unbearable. First they gave me powerful pain killers that were never really enough. Then I was put in a wheelchair for three months to see if that made any difference, but it didn't. It was clear that something drastic would have to be done.

Two of the top orthopaedic surgeons of the time, Donald Brooks and Austin Brown, came down to the children's home to examine me. They argued and argued about the best approach to take. Donald Brooks thought that it would be a terrible mistake to operate on my right foot since I had become very dextrous with it and used it as a hand. Austin Brown took the opposing view: that my mobility in the future would be even more important to me than using my feet as hands. They discussed it at great length but just couldn't agree.

I remember Ruth Cartwright, the head physiotherapist, saying to me, 'You're going to have to make a decision, Alison, because these two can't.' It was one of the very few times that I was ever allowed to make a decision about my own body or what was about to happen to me. I knew it was an experiment, an operation that had never been done before. But I also knew I had to do it, because I needed to be on my feet. In any case, I thought that they'd just turn my foot around and that I'd still be able to use it as a hand. I didn't realize that when the tendons and muscles were cut that would be it. I would never get the movement back in the foot that I used to have before I had the operation. And I would have to switch to using my mouth to hold things instead of my feet.

It was one of the most traumatic experiences of my life. I went in the day before the operation basically quite independent and I woke up the next day, in the recovery room, flat on my back. This may sound strange, but it was like becoming disabled for the first time. Before I'd been mobile and could do most things with my feet, now I was completely unable to move or do anything for myself. And the pain! I had fifteen pethidine injections during the course of the first night and many more during the following weeks. In the end, they had to take me off it, because they said I was going to become addicted. I had no concept of the pain that I was going to put myself through.

I don't think I had a breakdown but I certainly was desperately depressed. I just lay there thinking, 'Shit, what have I done? This is it. I've fucked myself up for ever.'

They sent Nurse Shepherd to sit with me to cheer me up. She was the only one who could console me during my first week of recovery. But the nursing staff were really supportive as well and as I got to know them my spirits slowly lifted. I was in the recovery ward for eight months. Every month seemed like a year, but at a certain point I realized that I *was* eventually going to be well enough to get out of there. That thought kept me going.

The operation on my foot had left me even more trapped in a wheelchair but I knew that I must learn to walk again. For me mobility meant freedom, escape. I think that's what made me fight, has always made me fight – the strong desire to be independent.

One day I was well enough to return to upper dorm and both Tara and I were delighted to discover that we had been given a room of our own to share. We had become seniors by then, which brought a new set of privileges. We were allowed to stay up until ten o'clock to watch television. I remember being crazy about *Hill Street Blues*.

They had placed Tara and me in different houses when we were five, probably in the hope that we would not be such close friends and always in each other's company. There were two houses; I was in one while Tara was in the other. The house system was common in boarding schools, and there was a constant competition between the two houses. Children could be awarded house marks for good work and good behaviour and at the end of the term the house with the most marks won the house trophy.

We also had sports days, which were just like sports days at any other school. There were running and swimming races, the high jump, long jump and javelin – in fact, all events which they had in the Olympic Games – and you could enter any of them if you thought you were capable.

I was not particularly sporty but I was a very good swimmer and broke a British record at Stoke Mandeville when I was sixteen. I love swimming and the good swimmers like Pete, Tara and myself gave up our lunch hours to train. At that time I was as good as they were and, on occasion, could beat both of them, but I didn't pursue it and they went on to compete at international level, while I took another direction and became an artist.

The separation by house meant that during our time at the home Tara and I were, to some extent, pitted against each other mentally and physically. Neither of us liked it and it didn't make us better children or better adults, but that was the situation. As far as school work was concerned Tara won easily. She was very intelligent and academically inclined whereas I had dyslexia and found school work difficult. When I got my files recently I read that my backwardness in the classroom had been noted at the age of ten and they were worried about it. The notes even included a mention that it might be dyslexia but for some reason they never followed up that theory to find out if it was correct or not and I spent my classroom years categorized as academically backward. Many years later, when I was doing an art course in Hammersmith, they took a good look at my educational problems. I went to a special centre where I was assessed and it was finally acknowledged that I had dyslexia. But it was never diagnosed at the children's home and I was always in the slow learners' class while all my close friends like Tara and Simon were in the top class for the bright children. In fact, I didn't learn to read until I was twelve, which was in stark contrast to all my friends, who had been excellent readers from an early age.

The culture of a school can be very judgemental and divisive, especially among the children, and the home was no exception. My friends could easily have said to me: 'You're not in our class so you're not our friend.' But that never happened. They never made fun of me or alluded in a negative way to the fact that I was in the slow learners' class. I wonder now how I managed to hold my own with them, how I gained their friendship and respect even though I was not academically their equal. Perhaps intellectual ability and braininess were not everything. Perhaps adventurousness, drive and determination compensated for my lack in those areas. Socially I more than held my own, it was just school work that I was no good at.

In October 1979, when I was fourteen, I was in my school classroom doing an English lesson when Jill Rocky walked in. We all looked up and wondered what was going on. She was the head of occupational therapy so I knew her, but it was unusual for her to come into a class like that. Normally a meeting would have been scheduled well in advance and would take place outside school hours.

'Alison, could you come with me, please. I'd like you to meet someone.' She wouldn't tell me who it was so my curiosity got greater and greater with each step as we walked along together to her office.

The 'someone' was a tanned good-looking man in a suit waiting for us in her office. I assumed he was a prospective visitor or a donor of funds, but whoever he was didn't matter because he got me out of the classroom – and I still relished the occasions when I got to meet somebody new. I said hello and he introduced himself as Mike from East London, South Africa. Five months earlier his wife had given birth to a baby girl, Nicky, in a hospital there. He showed me the photographs he had taken and I saw that the baby looked very similar to how I had looked at the same age. She was missing both arms and had short legs like me. I was instantly drawn to the story of Nicky and Mike. I was fascinated that Nicky's impairments were so similar to mine but I was equally struck by Mike himself. He looked me straight in the eye and spoke in a quiet, sincere voice. He didn't patronize me or jolly me along or pat me on the head. And it didn't take long for me to realize how steadfastly and utterly committed he was to his baby daughter's welfare.

We sat down together and drank tea, and Mike told me what had happened. His wife, Margie, had had a normal pregnancy – it was her second child – and she went into hospital to have the baby expecting to have a straightforward delivery. Mike had been there all through the labour and he was still

112

present when the baby was born. But he could tell by the look on the doctor's face that all was not well. The doctor called him over and explained that the new baby did not have all her limbs. He was very sorry and didn't know what the cause might have been. Mike stood there dumbstruck. Nicky was taken from the delivery room for examination to see if there were any other complications and neither Mike nor Margie was able to see or hold her until the following day. Mike described walking slowly back towards Margie and sitting down at the edge of her bed. He tried to explain to her as gently as possible what the doctor had said about the nature of Nicky's physical condition. Margie lay there speechless while she listened to Mike's words. She told me later, when I finally got to meet her, that she just stared blankly back at him because she was in shock. They both were. She remembers Mike getting up, going over to the window and standing there for what seemed like hours. He was watching the traffic lights changing from green to amber to red over and over again.

It had been completely unexpected. South Africa had no history of thalidomide cases and the hospital medical staff had no experience with babies like Nicky. They were at a complete loss and could give Mike and Margie no advice as to how best they might look after her. It looked hopeless, but Mike remembered reading a newspaper article about the thalidomide problem and the next day he went to his local library to see what he could find out about Nicky's condition and saw a mention of our children's home in England. When he got home he decided to write them a letter of inquiry asking for help and advice.

113

Jill Rocky, also a South African, wrote back to say that they had a great deal of expertise in this particular field and if he was in England he was welcome to visit. She also said that they had a child at the home, an older girl, who was a lot like Nicky.

Mike continued with his story and I listened utterly fascinated. I found the idea that there was somebody else who had been born with the same impairments as me extremely compelling, but even more than that I was completely caught up in hearing how Mike and Margie had responded to the situation they had found themselves in. As he continued talking in his soft measured voice I found myself thinking how different their attitude was compared to my mother's.

The two South Africans were upset and emotional but Mike told me they never thought for a moment that they would send Nicky to a home. They were adamant that she would remain in their care. The hospital staff were helpful and supportive of their decision and Nicky went home with them the next day. She began to be breast-fed straightaway and became part of family life. They never left her at home but took her out and about with them from day one so that she had a normal family life.

He then asked me some questions about myself. How long had I been at the institution? How did I dress myself? He wanted to get an idea of how they could help Nicky to best prepare her for adulthood. But I could tell that he was interested in me personally as well. He wasn't just going through the motions to get the information that he wanted.

After tea we took Mike for a guided tour and I think he

was impressed by many things, especially how competent a lot of us were in coping with our everyday environment.

A year later he came back for a second visit and brought Margie and little Nicky. By then I was sharing a room with Tara and we were both there when Mike knocked on our door. I took Nicky under my wing and paid her a lot of attention. She constantly followed me round as I demonstrated various movements of mine such as getting on and off the bed and picking up things and drawing some figures in crayon using my mouth; in fact, a good selection of my whole repertoire of skills and abilities which I'd learned during my fifteen years at the home. I spoke to her in that cooing singsong that I had heard adults using when they communicated with babies and toddlers and Nicky responded very well to me.

Mike and Margie booked themselves into a hotel in the local town and they brought Nicky in to spend the day with us. They wanted Nicky to be exposed to Tara and me so that she would see and perhaps copy some of our skills. Naturally, I was very happy to help and saw Nicky as a kind of baby sister.

On their last night at the hotel, Mike and Margie invited Tara and I out for a meal and naturally we never refused invitations like that. They asked us where we wanted to go and we said the local Wimpey restaurant, please. That was the top of the tree for Tara and I as far as restaurants were concerned. Mike and Margie were intrigued to see the kind of establishment we had chosen to be taken out to. I'm sure they were very disappointed when we sat down and they got their first look at the menu. But they didn't show it. Tara and I happily ordered burgers and fries and a milkshake each. We felt like we were at the Ritz and when the food arrived we showed our enthusiasm by eating as if we hadn't eaten for days. Mike and Margie intently watched us the whole time and I remember thinking that we were doing something wrong in the way we were eating. I was racking my brains to see what element of our etiquette was missing. Was there something Miss Barton had taught us that I was forgetting? In fact, I was way off the mark. Mike told me many years later that watching Tara and I eat our meal so adeptly was a specially uplifting experience for them. They were inspired and encouraged by our confidence and skill and, seeing how well we coped, knew that Nicky would be able to cope just as well when she was older.

Although they took both Tara and me out for a meal that day, it was my relationship with them that developed more strongly. Initially, I think I was a more useful model for them to observe because I more closely resembled Nicky than Tara did. Seeing how I went about things gave them better clues as to how they might help Nicky in the future and I was also able to tell them a lot about my life and how I coped with everyday challenges. But there was also a greater natural bond between us and that continued to develop. Mike and his family returned to Windsor after a few days, but a week later Mike returned because they wanted to take me to see *Evita*. Mike took me all the way to London in a taxi. I had never been to a West End show and I was entranced by the intensity and scale of the spectacle.

At the end of the evening it was too late to return to the

home so we drove to Windsor and they smuggled me into their hotel room for the night. I loved the excitement of our evening in the West End and the luxury of staying in a hotel. It was in total contrast to my life at the home and I knew which of the two I preferred.

I didn't see my South African friends for another seven years but we kept in touch by letter and exchanged birthday and Christmas cards. They were unswerving in their friendship, even though we had met only a few times.

When Tara and I were sixteen our house mother told us that a policeman was coming to visit the senior children and that he would be giving us a talk. His name was Roger and he was from the local constabulary which was twinned with Dallas in Texas. We were to show him round and make him tea. They were celebrating a twenty-five-year anniversary of some kind and had decided to do something special for it. They were going to choose two children from the home and take them to Dallas for ten days of sightseeing and holidaymaking. He was meant to be appraising all the senior kids so that he could decide who would be the most suitable and deserving to go on the trip. Later that day the headmaster called us into his office and told us it would be Tara and I who were going on the trip. I am not sure why he picked us. I suppose we were outgoing, fairly polite and didn't look too bad. We were also a very practised double act and had been best friends throughout our time together. We had done our best to please him when he gave us his talk and our efforts must have made an impression.

You can imagine the effect the prospect of the trip to Dallas had on Tara and me. We were beside ourselves with excitement. It was something quite beyond the realms of possibility. We had seen the television series so that's what we thought it would be like.

We travelled in business class on British Caledonian Airways and the crew treated us like royalty. They allowed us to sip a little champagne and visit the captain in his cockpit.

We arrived in Dallas in the middle of the night and the heat hit us both like a brick wall. A car was waiting for us and we were taken to a house in the suburbs. The owners were Jim and Doris Fleming. He was a big tall man with a shock of grey hair, a real Texan. Doris was petite with dark hair and glasses. She was a real estate agent and Jim had worked for the FBI. They made us both feel very welcome and our disabilities and the way we must have looked had no effect on them at all.

I can't remember why we were staying with them but I suspect there was a church connection. They were keen churchgoers and their neighbours, whose swimming pool we were free to use, were as well. The Flemings introduced us to lots of people, all of whom were very kind and welcoming and loved our English accents. They were all churchgoers, too. We were both struck by the fact that nobody showed any shock or horror when they met us. The only time we saw Jim and Doris at all perturbed was when our driver from the police department arrived to take us out. His name was Dwayne and he was black. He stood on the doorstep and we saw from the

Flemings' pained expressions that he wasn't altogether welcome in the house. We had no such qualms about his colour and soon developed massive and competing crushes on Dwayne. He very graciously put up with two silly teenage girls around him all day.

Everywhere we went it seemed that the people couldn't do enough for us. We went to a baseball game and an American football game where we met the Dallas Cowboys. We went to a rodeo, a theme park and a pizza restaurant where people ordered pizzas as big as wagon wheels and then proceeded to eat them, every last slice. They took us to Nieman Marcus, a department store like Harrods in London. The chairman of the company met us at the door and we were taken to every department, given gold earrings and cowboy hats and cowboy dresses with buckskin fringes. I was captivated and entranced by Dallas. Everything was big, larger than life.

The third day of our stay was a Sunday and Dwayne suggested that we go with him to the Baptist church that he attended. Tara and I loved it. The choir was a very polished and swinging gospel ensemble. We had never seen anything like it before and the participation and joyful energy of the congregation made the service whizz by.

All too soon it came to an end. We were at the airport saying goodbye to Jim and Doris and feeling a little sad. Tara and I both knew we were returning once more to the ordinary everyday life of the children's home – definitely not our first choice holiday destination. But we were used to it. All our lives we had been given brief glimpses into other worlds. I had always relished those occasions, embraced the opportunities that came my way, but they were always temporary. Even my visits home had that quality. Only the children's home seemed a permanent place, the one fundamental structure in my life.

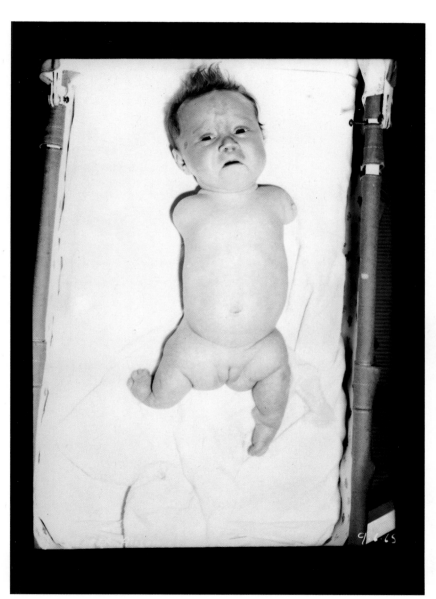

Me at three months old.

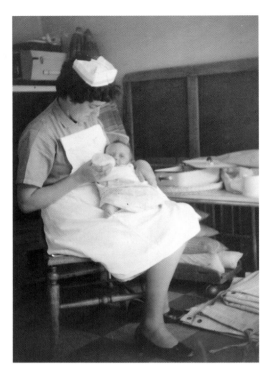

Being fed by a nurse.

With the other children at the children's home.

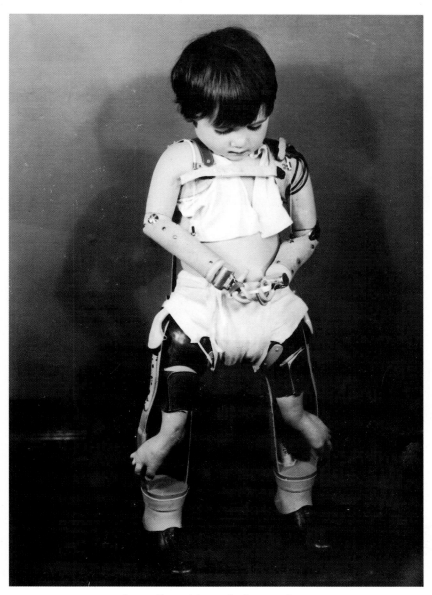

Struggling with my limb extensions.

Blowing bubbles with the Tates, the family who nearly adopted me.

At four years old, with Mum and Alan.

With Nurse Susannah on my fifth birthday. Notice the cake in the shape of an artist's palette.

With Pete.

With Nicky, a South African girl.

Me at Banstead at seventeen.

With Tara.

My mother and grandmother either side of me at my twenty-first birthday. My fiancé, Fran, stands behind my mother and Alan is behind my grandmother.

Winning a medal at the children's home.

Learning to ride with Mike and Janet.

In my specially adapted car.

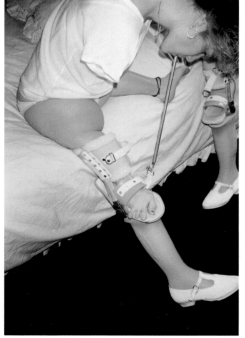

Using my dressing sticks. By this stage I was living in my own flat in London.

Wedding bells.

With Simon at a student Halloween party whilst at Brighton.

With friends in my flat in London, in the 1980s.

At twenty-eight I graduated from Brighton University.

This is me at my degree show.

Happy times in South Africa.

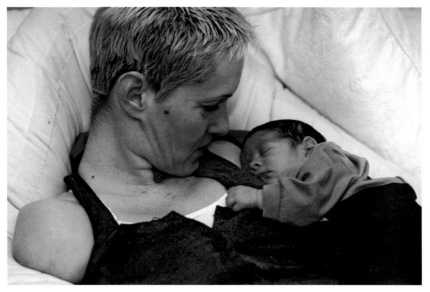

Parys and me.

Faces; some of my artwork.

Angel.

Getting an MBE for services to art.

With Parys.

Parys and the statue.

7

Boyfriends

Re ALISON LAPPER, Conference, 26th November, 1976 (4th review)

Age 11.7/12. Address: .... Yardley, Birmingham.

Diagnosis: 4-limb Dysmelia. Basically we decided to have a discussion about Alison because of some recent letters and events at upper dorm, and people are concerned about her

---

and her relationship with Ian [not his real name]. The letters themselves have really been dealt with.

<u>Nursing Officer Dormitory Units:</u> This relationship has been going on for a good 18 months. Night Sister has been very concerned about it.

<u>Deputy Head:</u> 18 months ago I reported that Alison and Ian's attitude was odd. I have found them together far more than is usual between friends and Ian is very deeply disturbed about it.

<u>Psychologist:</u> This is an unusual relationship because of the gap in ages. However they are both deprived children. Personally I do not think we have any hard evidence that anything improper is going on. As soon as I mentioned to Alison that we were old friends and I'd heard she might be in some sort of trouble she burst into tears and sobbed throughout the interview. She looked absolutely horrified when I suggested there had been any below waist activities and said 'Why can't they leave us alone? I just want to be friends.' In my opinion this is a relationship which may very well be supportive, and, if they have to be watched, this must be done in a caring and compassionate way. I think Alison is a very little girl – you have only to see her playing

so well with her dolls. It would do incalculable damage to Alison if we were to send her away. See if we can reconcile Alison and her mother. If we moved Alison or Ian now I think you could say goodbye to Ian's chances for his exams. He is so disturbed he would just 'blow'.

Physiotherapist: We have tried – so *hard* over the years to get Alison's parents more interested and caring.

Medical Social Worker: This relationship is unusual, especially on Ian's side because he is seeking comfort or friendship from someone much younger, but this is because he cannot cope with someone his own age. I raised the question of Ian being a day child during a home visit. He was against it and his mother was definitely against the idea. Physically he looks after himself, but at home he does not integrate and his mother finds this a problem.

Dr McCarthy pointed out that Alison is very immature physically, and although she may say things that sound worrying her understanding is much less. I think Ian is very disturbed and both children are very deprived. He is certainly a very mixed up boy; on the other hand he will only be with us until July 1977 and he is not here at weekends. Alison is desperately looking for affection and probably does not know what she's doing to Ian, but to remove her would be very damaging. I gather her family is pretty unsupportive and critical. Ian does not relate to any men because he's never had a good image of a father; he is smothered by his mother.

Chaplain/Warden: This is part of a much larger pattern which is emerging at the moment, and a number of staff have been very worried. I was very heavy-handed about this. Ian is not just interested in Alison. We encourage them to mix as much as possible. Ian is a very rough diamond and the product of a difficult background and I could not trust him ad lib. We have a tremendous responsibility at upper dorm and if anything were to happen parents would be down on us immediately. There are so many children that it is difficult to supervise them and get to know what is really happening without being heavy-handed.

Headmaster: A year ago the staff thought Alison was in moral danger, and everything I've seen during this last year has confirmed me in my belief that she is in moral danger. But everything has come to a head because of false evidence. Alison has always been keen on the boys and I realised that we should keep an eye on her. She has now moved into a new class. I do not seek to punish her, but I think she is a danger to herself. Ian is working hard and should do quite well in his CSE exams. I think we should put the day boy idea forward as a stage in integrating Ian into the community.

Child Psychiatrist: Alison was talkative throughout her interview and told me she came here when she was a few weeks old and on the whole was reasonably happy here. She sometimes gets fed up, mostly during the weekends, but expressed great gratitude for what we had done for her and said she worries about the future. She said one of her best friends had left recently – Peter Hull – and she misses him a lot. She spoke of the difficulties she encounters during her visits home; she feels she is now too heavy for her parents to lift her to the toilet. When I asked her whether she wanted to ask any questions she asked me whether I knew the cause as to why she was born with limb deficiencies. She has considerable anxiety about her birth and her future; the latter seems rather early. I will review Alison in three months.

School report: Alison has only been in my class for three months, but she is a delightful girl who is very popular and seemed to get on with everyone. She has a happy disposition and is cheerfully helpful and cooperative in every way.

She's interested in most schoolwork and puts much effort into it. She's over conscious of weakness in reading and spelling and is making great strides in the former. There are signs that she is gaining confidence in all directions and that should result in a quicker rate of progress. Alison has initiative and ingenuity, but thrives on encouragement and praise. I gather that in the past she has been depressed by criticism or correction, particularly if she felt it was over correction! She still needs caring attention but is less touchy and more philosophical about criticism; she's growing up and interested in the process. She has great sensitivity to colour, music and movement and when doing movement to music she lets the music take over. She loves to draw, particularly tall girls with long legs and arms. During lessons on growing things Alison's questions are directed to the animal and human rather than plants, insects, etc.

RECOMMENDATIONS:
1. Dr Lena to see Ian
2. M.S.W. to arrange for Ian's mother to see Dr Lena
3. Dr McCarthy to write to Alison's parents inviting them to the bungalow on the grounds that unless we can have some more contact with them it is very difficult for us to look after Alison.

cc. Headmaster; Chaplain/Warden; Dr Lena; Psychologist; Medical Social Worker

I had reviews like this every year during my time at the home. It gives a very good idea of the kinds of attitudes towards us which prevailed among the various professionals at the time. It also shows very clearly the gulf that existed between how we were seen by the teachers at the school and how we were seen and dealt with by the other staff in the domestic part of our lives. In this confidential report most of the concern and focus was on my relationship with a boy called Ian. We were both inmates and had become friends when he was thirteen and I was nine. He was sweet, patient and funny and we got on well. I enjoyed his attention and didn't read anything into a four-year difference in ages. In the early stages of our friendship the staff thought it was a big joke because of the age difference and because we were disabled. Neither of us minded that because we were used to the staff teasing us in that petty kind of way. But none of the kids ever teased us. All of us 'crips' – that's what we called ourselves – were very solid, very loyal to each other. And it was always us against the staff.

Ian and I met every day after school and chatted and hung out together. And once in a while Ian would manage to get a kiss out of me. He was getting old enough to want a little kissing but I wasn't interested at that age. It was all very innocent.

By the time I was eleven and he'd just turned sixteen we

127

were still going out together and had established a strong relationship. I didn't think the difference in our ages was at all strange and we both had a very different perspective on our friendship compared to the comments made by the care staff in their report. It was certainly more of a romantic association than a physically sexual one, at least on my side. But we flirted and alluded to sex because we were young and interested in it, and it was in the air by that time. Since we didn't see each other quite as much as we would have liked and because there was very little physical activity going on between us, we compensated by writing each other romantic letters. I didn't know much about writing lovey-dovey letters so I got help from a friend, Lucy, the daughter of an electrician working at the home. She would come down to my dorm and we'd sit there giggling and making up things about condoms; stuff I mostly knew nothing about. Ian would get my letter the next day and then he'd write me one back. I knew that my letters meant a lot to him because of his enthusiastic responses but I didn't realize he was keeping them all in his locker. It was a crazy thing to do because the home was not a place where they allowed you any privacy. In that regard it was more like a prison than a home. The staff felt entitled to go through your locker and search your things whenever they wanted. And they did, usually when you were elsewhere on the site. It didn't happen immediately but after a month or two they found the letters which I had written to Ian. The letters were confiscated and read by a succession of members of staff as they were passed up the line to higher and higher authority, finally ending up on the desk of the headmaster. The confidential review clearly shows that he was one of those types extremely concerned with the 'moral danger' which the young people in his charge were constantly threatened by. Along with that notion went a whole raft of ideas about discipline and social standards and being a good girl or a good boy. Sexual activity of any kind, but especially anything 'below the waist', was considered absolutely the worst kind of immoral behaviour.

The general view among the staff was that we shouldn't be thinking about sex at all. Having the kinds of impairments that we all exhibited meant in their eyes that it was our duty to turn our backs on any possibility of sex. It was a very prejudiced view which had two particular components. Firstly, they thought we were too repulsive physically for anyone able-bodied to possibly consider us attractive sexually. Secondly, there was something so fundamentally wrong about our shapes that it would not be right for us to contemplate any sexual activity even with each other, even if we felt the inclination and attraction. Ideally, we were meant to put that part of life aside.

That was the official line and it had a long list of supporters among the staff. But there was another factor that also came into play which was the fact that some of the staff – the male staff – clearly found some of the teenage girls to be cute and attractive and . . . sexy. Of course, they were absolutely forbidden to take any action but in those days staff were far less constrained in how much touching they were allowed to do while taking care of us. This gave ample opportunity for physical closeness and covert sexual rough and tumble. There was child–staff flirtation and members of staff were very friendly with teenage girls. The irony was that I was far from being one of those girls and apart from a little inept kissing I had no sexual experience at all. And I would continue to be in the dark about real sex until I went to live in London years later. But I had a high profile at the home and was very open and communicative. I had no particular skills in being secretive and hiding what I was really up to. If I was ever naughty I was always found out, and as I have said, was often blamed for things even when I had nothing to do with them.

The headmaster read the letters and it didn't take him long to decide that they represented a major outbreak of moral danger and that swift action needed to be taken if I were to be saved from the terrible fate which lay in store for me. At lunchtime that day all hell broke loose for Ian and myself. We were chatting in the dining room as we usually did when one of the wardens came through the door wearing a face like thunder. Most of the staff were brilliant at putting on these faces which combined anger, disapproval, disappointment and delight in the satisfaction of vengeful desire. They seemed to be saying: 'You're going to get it now, young lady, and not before time.' This particular warden was obviously enjoying himself: 'Alison Lapper! Ian! The head warden wants both of you in his office right now. They are all waiting.'

Ian and I couldn't figure out why we had been summoned. We knew that they didn't like our friendship but we had already been friends for two years and we had not been doing anything out of the ordinary. We didn't think about the letters. I didn't know they still existed and Ian assumed they were still safely stored in his locker. As we walked along the corridor trying to keep up with the warden who was escorting us, we both tried to work out what was going on and who the other people might be who were waiting for us in the head warden's office. We soon found out.

They separated us, and Ian went into the office first. Then it was my turn. I found myself before a board consisting of the headmaster, the warden, the deputy warden and just about everybody who had any rank. I sat down and the headmaster began questioning me in that odd rhetorical way which people in authority seemed to think was most effective. It was like a speech in a bad television drama. Did I know why I was there? Did I recognize the letters he held in his hand? Had I written those letters? What were they supposed to think? Had we been doing anything? We were to tell them everything and tell them the truth. They were convinced we'd been having sexual intercourse, as they called it. Of course, we hadn't and I said so, but they didn't believe me. I endured half an hour of back-and-forth questioning during which I repeatedly protested our innocence and they, just as determinedly, asserted our guilt. There was nothing that Ian or I could do or say that would satisfy them because our version of events didn't tally with their interpretation and they just didn't want to believe us.

Since neither Ian nor myself would 'confess', they took what was to them the next logical step to prove their case. Two days later, I was escorted to the medical unit for a medical examination. I couldn't decide whether I was more scared or angry. Why wouldn't they listen to us?

The doctor asked me to lie on the examining table and my knickers were removed by the nurse. I was then examined very thoroughly around my vagina. Medical examinations are meant to be forensic scientific procedures. They're supposed to be emotionally neutral and experienced as a necessary fact-gathering exercise. But I was feeling far from emotionally neutral. I felt ashamed and humiliated. Everyone had refused to believe the truth that I'd stated over and over again. And now the authorities were going to extreme lengths to prove themselves right. It was like being part of how I imagine a rape investigation is handled when the police are gathering their evidence. I assume they're much more sensitive and careful in the way they deal with rape victims than the staff were with me that day.

The doctor shone the overhead light and continued her probing and examining. That year my periods had started and I had been trying to come to terms with this new development in my body. The staff had been training me to insert a tampon for myself and Peter Tutt had designed a jointed metal dressing stick with a row of prongs at the end which I was supposed to operate with my shoulder. His wife, Margaret, was meant to have tried it out beforehand to make sure it worked. But it wasn't the easiest manoeuvre in the world to perform because I couldn't see what I was doing and it was very hard to get the tampon to stay on the prongs. It would keep falling off or the angle wouldn't be right and I was a little red in that area from mismanaged attempts.

The redness was all the proof they needed. Nothing we said did any good and the full force of institutional wrath came down on us. We were forbidden to meet, talk or even look at each other. It was not so bad for Ian. He was a quiet rebel and didn't give a damn what they did or said. And he was leaving soon anyway. But I had six years to go and the home was still my life. I felt shamed and humiliated by the whole incident, especially the fact that few believed us. And for the first time the kids didn't rally round and back us up against the staff. When I walked to school the next day, one of the girls hissed at me: 'I don't know how you can show your face in here!'

In a final twist we were both forced to have a series of separate sessions with a psychotherapist. They were everything I had always imagined such sessions would be like. I would lie on the bed in my dormitory and she would try to put me at ease. She seemed like a nice person and very professional. She asked me questions about the home and about myself. Was I happy? How did I feel about my disability? Did I ever feel angry?

She also had a long list of words on a bit of paper and would read them out one by one. As she said each one I was supposed to respond by saying out loud the first word that came into my head. It was the association game. If she said 'orange' I might say 'squash'. Then at some point she would say 'Ian' and, no doubt, I was supposed to reply 'sex' or something like that. But I didn't. I think I said 'friend' in response to that one. As I spoke she would write down what I said in her notes and we would carry on like that for about forty minutes. It seemed pretty pointless to me but maybe she was able to find out all kinds of clever things about my personality using her years of psychiatric training and experience. If she did, she never told me what they were.

After two months the sessions came to an end and, from my point of view, were an inconclusive exercise. I do remember that the one thing the therapist didn't ask me about was my mother.

8

Banstead

My final two years at the home were my best. First I was made captain of my house, while Tara was made captain of hers. We were now prefects and could inhabit a new domain of our own called the castle. The castle had a pool table and comfy chairs and was a private retreat for the prefects alone. We had tea and coffee facilities in there and most importantly it was warm and private, and adults could only enter with our invitation. No more hanging about and freezing outside in the yard the way we had to when we were juniors. Simon was made chief librarian and a prefect. He was in the castle with us, and it became a tradition that he always made the tea.

When we became prefects our behaviour also changed.

———

We were still cheeky and retained a lot of our old 'attitude', but we were aware that we were meant to be setting an example to the juniors and, on the whole, that's what we did. In my last year I was made head girl and Tara was my deputy. And we ruled the roost together, still very much the best of friends.

My school work improved, as did my self-confidence. I won an external art competition as well as two major school awards. And my mobility was much better since the operation a few years earlier. My parents even came down from Birmingham for Speech Day to see me receive my two school prizes and I thought I almost saw my mother on the verge of expressing some words of praise and congratulation. It was a golden time but it was drawing to a close.

For seventeen years I had lived there. It was my home and all my friends were there. I had the respect of the staff. I was head girl. I had finally got a grasp of how things worked and could often, though not always, manipulate things to my advantage. I had learned who liked me and who didn't, and how not to upset certain people. I had even grown to like being there. But every child had to leave the home when they reached the age of sixteen. That was the rule. I had already been there an extra year because of my operation and now that year was up. It was time for me to go. That meant leaving all my friends, my familiar situation, my whole world. I said I didn't want to go. They said I had to. I talked to members of staff whom I trusted and asked them to help me to stay on. They explored the possibilities as best they could but one by one they came back to me and said that it was not possible. I looked for loopholes, anything that would have allowed me to stay, but there weren't any. And so my last day arrived. It was 21 June 1982.

Tara helped me pack my things. There wasn't much. We fitted everything that I had accumulated during my seventeen years into a small suitcase and two bin bags. She was saddened and tearful. We had been like two peas in a pod since I was two, inseparable best friends. Now she would get a new roommate and I would be gone. It was a strange thing but I didn't feel so bad. I was almost cheerful, or at least pretending to be. I had gradually got used to the idea that I would have to leave the children's home and I had convinced myself it was the start of a great new adventure.

At twelve o'clock two of the staff came into our room. One said, 'The minibus is here, Alison. It's time to go. I'll get your things.'

They picked up my bin bags and suitcase and we all walked in a little group towards the mahogany doors that opened on to the outside. We were chatting cheerfully. They said they'd miss me. I said I'd miss them. We continued along the corridor in a light, carefree mood and one of the staff went ahead through the doors to hold them open for me. As I crossed the threshold I looked out and saw the white minibus waiting in the drive about sixty yards away. It was a sunny day, not a cloud in the sky, and the driver had the special door, the tailgate type that lowers for wheelchairs and disabled people, open and ready at the back of the minibus. I looked across the green to that familiar tailgate door – I had been in the minibus so many times before – and something inside my head flipped. I was suddenly scared and angry and completely overpowered by a feeling of utter panic. I turned and raced back towards the building, desperate to get back to the safety and security of my only home, but they caught up with me in a couple of strides. As they grabbed me I started shouting and screaming and swearing at the staff.

'Let me go! I don't want to go. I'm *not* going. Don't make me go. Please . . . please don't make me go!'

I was using all my strength and every trick I could think of to evade their grasp and get back inside. But they easily picked me up and bundled me on to the minibus. By the time they had sat me in my seat and put on my seat belt, all the fight in me had gone. The driver started the engine and we slowly pulled out of the drive. Perhaps they were waving goodbye to me as we drove out of the gates. I don't know. I was writhing and shaking with great shuddering sobs, my head buried in the side of the seat. One of the staff acted as my escort on this journey and they probably did their best to comfort me, but I was oblivious. I cried for most of the drive to Banstead. We were travelling through some of the most beautiful countryside in England but I didn't notice. I felt numb and my mind was a blank. I wrapped myself in my desolate mood and stared out of the window, seeing nothing. Some time later we arrived at my new home.

Queen Elizabeth's Foundation for Disabled People had an assessment centre at Banstead in Surrey. And that's where the minibus took me. The centre trained disabled people so that they could live in the outside world on the best possible terms. After we were trained to look after ourselves, to do all the daily tasks that non-disabled people could do, they assessed us to see whether we were capable of living on our own, needed some kind of sheltered accommodation that provided some help and assistance, or needed to go back into an institution to be cared for by a full-time professional staff.

I didn't like Banstead from the first moment I saw it. It was an institution like my children's home, but somehow blander and duller. The buildings were uninteresting and it smelled of that familiar combination: disinfectant, boiled cabbage and stale clothes.

My escort helped with my bin bags and suitcase and we made our way to the nurse's station to register my arrival. I could tell immediately that this was yet another place where the staff exerted power over the residents and bowed and scraped to the hierarchy above them. I didn't like that and I didn't know anybody there. Also, I was a new arrival and would have to start all over again from the bottom of the heap. Whichever way I looked at it seemed bad to me. They must have noticed my mood but didn't say anything. I was shown to my room and left there. I had one or two perfumes, a little bit of make-up, and some clothes which I put in the wardrobe. I had some pictures, posters and a single-deck record player that had belonged to my sister, and I had my singles and LPs. Those were my belongings after seventeen years at the home.

I had to share my room with another person, but I can't remember them at all. We all took our meals in a large refectory and that's where I went for my first lunch. I think I was still in a state of shock over the enormity of the change that had taken place in my life. The next day and the day after that I struggled to come to terms with my new situation. I went through the motions of going to the classes where they assessed my abilities in various categories. But essentially I was not complying, not doing what they wanted. I wasn't interested. There were thirty or forty other disabled young people there but I wandered round in a daze and spoke to nobody. I had no friends because I kept aloof, and soon gained a reputation for being a snob. I don't know why but I was finding it extremely difficult to adjust to Banstead and its peculiarities. I should have been used to the ways of institutions and the personnel that ran them after seventeen years, but in the first few months Banstead was too much for me.

For instance, there was the head cook. She seemed to hold a position of power way beyond her role. She would get all the staff together and they would all have a big moan about how badly we behaved and treated them. Then a monthly meeting would be organized. All the students and the care staff would have to attend. And the cook would be in charge of the proceedings. She would read out from a list of misdemeanours student by student. It would be things like: You haven't been eating what I've been giving you. You haven't done your washing properly. You haven't got the right attitude. All the transgressors would get a dressing down one by one, even for the most trivial things. They treated us as if we were eight years old. I couldn't believe it. I used to sit there with my mouth open wondering who these people were and how they had come to be like this. It was so petty. It was verging on the bizarre.

I should add that in due course the cook left and the new cook, Graham, was a nice guy, and very good at his job. And that was the end of the monthly meetings.

Another practice at Banstead, which I resented deeply,

was the way in which they charged us for just about every-thing. We each had an individual weekly allowance from the government and we had to pay out of it for various individual items such as our washing, stationery, writing and artist's materials, more or less anything they could assign a monetary value to and charge us for. As part of our independence train-ing they were trying to teach us about money and how to handle it. We were each given a set of little brown envelopes. Every month we would receive our various bills. We checked our bills and filled each envelope with the appropriate sums of money from our allowance: laundry money, swimming money, stationery money, and so on. And at the end of each month they collected up all the little brown envelopes and we would get a new set. By the time all these small payments had been taken out of our allowance there was virtually nothing left for us to spend. I suppose they wanted us to learn what it would be like in real life but I always thought of it as an unnecessary rip-off. After all, the cost of my stay at Banstead was being paid for in full by Birmingham Council.

The staff at Banstead didn't like my attitude, and I was regularly called into one office or another to receive a talking to. It was strange at the time and seems even stranger when I look back on it now. On one occasion, when I was called in, I found myself sitting face to face with a man of about sixty, a social worker. He was sitting on the other side of his desk and continued reading through my file for a few minutes without looking up. I could see that there was something slightly odd about him but I couldn't work out what. When he had finished reading he looked up and I realized what it was. He was wearing a grey toupee and whenever he talked or moved his head the toupee would move into a slightly different position. It almost had a life of its own and I couldn't take my eyes off it. Meanwhile, he read me brief extracts from a number of negative reports that people had made about me.

'Well?' he said.

'Well?' I said.

He gave me a sour look followed by a long lecture. I was being too aloof and my expectations were far too great. I had issues. I needed to sort myself out. I needed to pull my socks up. What with? I thought.

I wanted to shout: 'You're the one with issues, mate! Look at that stupid toupee. Everyone can see you're bald!' But I didn't, of course. The thing that really got me was that here was this man, from a totally different generation, trying to tell me how to live my life. What could he possibly know about an 18-year-old girl with no arms who'd spent her whole life in an institution?

Not long after my arrival I became depressed and began to think of only one thing: how I could leave Banstead.

I had been in telephone contact with my mother and she knew I was unhappy there. She said that if I hated it so much at Banstead, why didn't I come home to live with her and Alan. I was so low at the time that moving back to my mother's home in Birmingham seemed an appealing possibility. I talked to the staff at Banstead about it and after a few weeks they arranged a case conference to discuss what was the best thing to do about my future. The meeting took place in a large office at

Birmingham Council's education department. There were social workers from my children's home, from Banstead, from Birmingham, as well as education officers and representatives from other bodies. My mother and I were also present.

It was a long meeting and a number of possibilities were discussed in great detail. But in the end it all boiled down to either staying at Banstead or going home to live with my mother. Everyone around the table had had their say and now they all turned and looked at me. I was surprised. I had fully expected that this group of professional case workers would come to some kind of decision as a result of their own deliberations and I would have to abide by it. But it now became clear that it was going to be entirely up to me what I chose to do. I didn't answer immediately. During the discussions my mother had been questioned about whether she really wanted me back in her home and whether she would be able to cope and make the necessary adjustment to my being there. Apart from anything else she would have to allow an extensive modification to the house to enable me to function in that environment. For example, all the door handles would have to be lowered so I could reach them and the locks changed so that I could let myself in and out of the house. The kitchen would have to be modified so that I could prepare my own meals when necessary. And I would need a special bath and toilet. My mother said that she was willing to make all the necessary changes, but I was watching her closely when she spoke and I found it hard to believe that she would allow her beautiful house to be adapted just for my benefit. It didn't ring true. Maybe I was doing her an injustice, but in any case I was entirely at her mercy in the matter and that's what scared me. If for some reason the modifications never happened I would be trapped in that house, only ever able to come and go and do things at my mother's convenience.

There were other factors, too. It dawned on me that if I moved back home I wouldn't be able to learn to drive. I wouldn't be able to go to an able-bodied college and my dream of living an independent life as a self-determining human being would be over. So I looked up at the circle of waiting faces and said that I'd like to give Banstead another try.

I could see many looks of relief because they thought I was making the right choice. But as we were leaving, my mother said to me: 'I will never forgive you for that.'

'For what?'

'You were going to come and live at home and now you've decided to go back to Banstead.'

I really don't know what she meant but she said it with real intensity. Perhaps she really had wanted me to move back home and be permanently in the family. Perhaps she had hated attending the case conference and seeing all the various professionals discussing my welfare in such a public forum. Or maybe something else had upset her. I said, 'Ma, I need to be able to drive. I need to be able to take care of myself, to be independent before I can come home.' She didn't reply and we made the journey to her house in cold silence. We always seemed to be in conflict about one thing or another.

When I returned to Banstead after the case conference things miraculously changed. I started riding horses. Banstead had access to riding stables and all the students were given the opportunity to go riding. I knew about it but the whole idea of being on a horse scared me. It didn't make sense for somebody like myself with no arms to be on a horse. How would I hold on to the reins? How could I stop myself falling off? If the horse bolted I wouldn't stand a chance. I told them I wasn't interested, there was no way they were going to get me on a horse. But the head physiotherapist at Banstead was a fearsome woman called Anne Sandicot and she made me go. She made everyone go. We didn't have any choice. The only way anyone could get out of horse riding was if they were too heavy and since that didn't apply to me, off I went.

When I first arrived at the stables I quite liked seeing the horses and ponies. They looked pretty. I loved their big brown eyes and their long manes and tails. But I still didn't want to ride on one. I was taken to a pony one of the grooms had brought out, and left there to await my fate. The stables had a special wood block and the pony was led alongside it. I sat my bottom on the saddle and then swung my artificial leg over to the other side. So far so good, but my heart was thumping. One of the helpers put my feet in the stirrups and there I was – sitting on a pony. The next second the pony twitched its ear and the sudden movement freaked me out. I started screaming and, of course, that spooked the pony. They held it steady but I felt vulnerable, as if I might fall off at any moment. I just didn't like it and I was determined to make that the last time I ever got on a horse. But they were very patient with me, and firm. They led me at a slow walk round the sand school and after a few more visits to the riding stables I began to change my tune. It was a very gradual process but I slowly became more confident. The lady helpers, Muriel, Janet and Barbara, were very kind and we remain friends to this day. There was also an instructor called Mike who was excellent at teaching horsemanship. He and Janet taught me to hold the reins in my mouth and control the pony's movements in that way. I liked all four of them and developed a strong relationship with them. Soon I began to look forward to Thursday morning riding sessions. It was a real treat to get away from Banstead and spend time with my four new friends. In the beginning I never rode the pony, I simply sat on it. One person led the pony and two other people were either side of me to keep me steady and to catch me if I fell. Later on, I was allowed to ride on my own without being led or assisted in any way. Thanks to their efforts, and my own, I became quite good at riding.

The crucial piece of equipment for me was a special strap called the Huntington surcingle. I was tied on to the saddle with the strap and that kept me firmly in place so I was able to keep my balance and concentrate on guiding the pony by the reins, which were held in my mouth. I learned to do all the usual things like riding round little courses and in and out of cones. I became very adept. On one occasion I trotted up behind Mike, let go of the reins and pulled his cap off with my mouth. He couldn't believe that I'd managed that.

There was a little black pony called Winston who was assigned to me. He could never be ridden just behind other ponies because he would always upset them. So I either had to ride him a long way back or else right at the front. He wasn't an easy pony but I really enjoyed the challenge of keeping Winston under control and making sure he didn't upset the other horses.

The riding was not the only new development after the case conference in Birmingham. The assessment centre was keen for me to continue my further education and asked me what I would like to do. My dyslexia had still not been recognized and I was struggling with most of the subjects that I had to grapple with. The only thing I was good at, and which my dyslexia didn't affect, was art. Banstead decided that it would be good for me to go to an able-bodied college and study for my Art O-level. So I was enrolled in Sutton College of Learning for Adults.

It was going to be my first time doing a course in a normal able-bodied institution and I was petrified about going. One of the further education staff came with me for my first day at college. I was the only disabled person on the course and they were not used to having someone with my disabilities. Nothing was geared up for me and I spent most of the lesson fiddling about with easels and table heights. I was so embarrassed. But by the second day everything was sorted out. A taxi took me to the college in the morning and brought me back in the afternoon and when I started to get friendly with a couple of the students on my course my mood at Banstead improved considerably.

I realized that I needed to work hard and achieve things if I was to arrive at my main goal in life, which was to get out of care, to live a life outside an institution. I made some good friends at SCOLA, Jean and Joe and Claire and Matthew. I also started to get a real taste for the outside life, life outside Banstead. And I loved it.

My course finished at nine o'clock every evening. I was

supposed to go back to Banstead at that time but I rarely did. Instead, I went out with my new friends, clubbing and partying till late. Very often I would arrive back at Banstead at two or three in the morning, where the night duty staff would be waiting. They would have a go at me, asking me where I'd been and what time I thought this was but there was nothing they could do. The only action they could have taken would have been to stop me doing my course and that would have been a step too far. Suddenly the staff had no power over me and I revelled in my new freedom. I was regularly put into the report book for coming back late but that was as far as it went because fundamentally they wanted me to progress, to continue with my studies and my riding and swimming.

Having regular and free access to the outside world was a major change in my life. I began to get a clearer idea of how people lived and enjoyed their lives in the outside world and it made me more determined than ever to achieve my goals and get my independence.

At Banstead they had a specially designed flat where each of the disabled residents could spend some time learning how to cope with the challenges of being in the everyday world. It was meant to replicate the conditions we would have to deal with successfully in order to live in our own home one day. I was sitting in the training flat doing a drawing when I heard the door being opened. I looked up and a smart well-dressed man in his forties walked in. I had no idea who he was but he seemed very at ease and familiar with the surroundings. He introduced himself as Colin Smart and said that he was an architect who sometimes did work for Banstead and other similar organizations. I told him I was doing an Art O-level and had been interested in painting and drawing since I was three. We chatted on and I very quickly began to like him. He had a great sense of humour and I could tell that he was really interested in the problems that disabled people faced. He was also very practical and unsentimental. And, above all, he didn't patronize.

He asked me if I had ever been to an art gallery and I said that I hadn't.

'We'll have to do something about that.'

'And what might that be?'

'Have you ever been to the Royal Academy in London.'

'No. Never heard of it. What is it?'

'It's a very big gallery in London and their summer exhibition has just started. I think we should pay a visit, don't you?'

'What's a summer exhibition?'

He explained how thousands of amateur painters from all over Britain submitted their work with the hope of it being put on display at the Royal Academy. Very few were chosen. Naturally I loved the idea of going to see some of the best paintings by non-professional artists. I was one of those myself. Maybe I could submit a painting someday.

Colin Smart, although I didn't know it at the time, was going to play an important role in my bid to join society at large and live as an independent person within it.

There was one further crucial development in my life at Banstead and it was the most important of all. Jenny Pearce was an occupational therapist at Banstead who was assigned to me. In one of our talks together I tentatively asked her if there was any chance I might be able to learn how to drive a car. I expected a gently negative answer because I didn't see how it was possible for me to control a car safely. But she immediately said that she didn't see why not. And I could tell she meant it. Jenny was one of those professionals whom I have had the good fortune to meet from time to time and who have genuinely wanted me to be all that I can be and do all that I can do. When I came to do my driving assessment, I told Morag Cornwall, the head of that department, that I wanted to learn to drive. She explained what would have to be done. But it wasn't simple. I would have to buy a car first. Then it would have to be engineered and modified to allow me to drive it with the same control able-bodied drivers have. Both steps were expensive and I had no money.

However, Morag picked up on my keenness and that was all the encouragement she needed. She wrote to charity after charity to raise funds so that I would be able to purchase a car. Then she contacted various engineering firms until she found one that had the expertise to make the extensive adaptations I would need. But there was more that needed to be done. Morag made a further phone call and soon we had a visit from Peter Roke and his partner who were setting up a new engineering venture. They talked with me, took measurements and considered the problem of adapting a car so that I could use it. They were starting from scratch so it was impossible to be certain but they were confident that with a mixture of hydraulics and servo assistance they would be able to create what was necessary for me to be able to drive. It would be the first car of its kind to be modified so that I would be able to drive it. The engineers had to fit the servo mechanism that would allow me to slot my shoulder into a shoulder rest. Pushing forward with my shoulder would turn the steering wheel to the right and pushing backwards, to the left. The accelerator and brake mechanisms would consist of two power-driven levers brought up to a level where I could operate them with one of my feet, more or less like a normal car. Most importantly, the design needed to fit me like a glove otherwise it would be too dangerous for me to drive.

It was a sunny day with blue skies when my first car, my very own, arrived at Banstead on a trailer. It was a blue Mini Metro. I can't describe the feelings I had when I saw it. It meant so much to me because at last I would be free to go where I wanted when I wanted. I would have my own wheels. It was incredible. It was the first big thing I had ever owned. There was only one problem. I still couldn't drive.

Morag arranged for an ex-policeman, Tony Dance, to be my driving instructor. He was a very patient man and a first-class instructor, perfectly suited to the challenge of teaching someone with no arms how to drive a car. I now had four people in my corner encouraging me to practise my driving and pass my driving test – Colin, Tony, Morag and Jenny – but I honestly didn't need their encouragement by then. I had all the motivation I needed bubbling up inside me every day.

I had lessons with Tony every week for five months. He was a brilliant driving instructor. He never raised his voice and was extremely patient. Above all he was unflappable. On my first lesson I was driving along tentatively, worried about my speed, which was probably only twenty miles an hour, when a massive lorry came roaring round the corner. I was safely on my side of the road and he was on his, but I was so overawed by the size of the oncoming vehicle that I slammed on the brakes.

'What are you doing, Alison?' He spoke in a soft, gentle voice with just a hint of mocking humour about it. He had a way of saying things that made me determined not to make that particular mistake again but which never upset or disheartened me. In addition, when I did well he let me know. I noticed that as the weeks passed he talked less and less about my driving and more about other subjects. I must have been getting better. When I wasn't having a lesson with Tony my blue Mini Metro was parked in the mobility centre at Banstead. I wasn't allowed to drive it but they trusted me with the keys. So every weekend I used to get in the driving seat and spend hours listening to pop music on the radio. Occasionally I started the engine and revved it up, pretending I was driving down country lanes to faraway places. Finally, the day arrived for my driving test. Tony picked me up from Banstead and we drove to the driving test centre in Crawley. I sat in the car waiting while Tony went inside to tell the examiner that I had arrived. I was getting more and more nervous and by the time the examiner arrived with his clipboard I was convinced I was going to fail.

'Shall we proceed with the test, Miss Lapper?' He was very formal and stiff. As I attempted to carry out his directives I had difficulty controlling my nerves. His face was impassive, so I couldn't tell from his expression how I was doing. I know at one point I turned right when he asked me to turn left, and I made two other small mistakes. By the time we returned to the test centre I knew. Oh well, not everyone passed first time. I would just have to take a second test in a few weeks. Once we were stationary again the examiner tested me on my Highway Code. He made a few marks on his clipboard, then left the car and disappeared inside the test centre building. I sat in my seat feeling dejected and waited for Tony to emerge. I was so disappointed. But when I saw Tony walking towards the car his face told another story. I had passed – first time. I had a final lesson with him as I drove us back along the motorway. He had been totally committed to me and my quest to learn to drive, and, as he congratulated me yet again on passing, I realized how lucky I was to have had him as my instructor. During the next few days I drove my car endlessly. I just got in, started the engine, and drove without having any destination in mind. Tony had never permitted me to have the radio on during my driving lessons, but now I had it on permanently with the volume turned up full blast. I love listening to loud pop music while driving.

A week later Colin came by to congratulate me. I suggested we go to London to celebrate, except that this time he didn't have to take me in his car. I would take him in mine. People who have been passengers in my car know that I'm not fond of the slow lane and I got us both to London in record time. Luckily Colin is not a nervous passenger. I could only drive with my legs off so my procedure was to walk to the car, open the door, collapse into the passenger seat, unstrap my artificial limbs, then slide into the driving seat. And when I arrived at a destination I would have to strap them back on again one by one. It was very laborious but I had to do it that way.

I drove straight to a shoe shop in Chelsea and parked outside. By now, Colin had taken me on a few trips to London and I was forming a taste for expensive clothes and accessories. Although I couldn't buy most of what I liked, I still enjoyed window shopping and going inside the luxurious interiors of upmarket stores. On this occasion I had seen a pair of fabulously stylish leather boots in the window and wanted to look at them and try them on. I wasn't planning on buying them but with characteristic generosity Colin said he would get them for me as a reward for passing my driving test.

We entered the shop and one of the assistants came up and asked if she could help. Colin asked her for a pair of the boots in the window in my size and she went off to get them. She had seen that I had no arms but when she came back the fact that I was wearing artificial legs hit her for the first time. She knelt down to help me pull the boots on but she looked nervous and couldn't get started. After a minute, she looked up at me and said that she didn't think she could do it because she might hurt me. I told her not to worry because the legs were artificial and didn't feel any pain. I was trying to be funny so that she would laugh and relax, but she continued to hesitate. Colin, who could see how uncomfortable she still was, stepped in. He sat on the stool with my artificial legs over his shoulders trying to fit the new boots on to them. It wasn't going to be easy. I looked across to the shop window and noticed a small crowd had gathered outside and were watching him pull the boots on. I said: 'Colin, look over there.' He looked up. Moments later he was red as a beetroot with embarrassment but still gamely lacing up the boots. I have to admit that one of my great pleasures on our little expeditions together was to embarrass him as much as possible. He always took it in very good grace and I think in a way he enjoyed it.

When we got back to the car I had to take my artificial legs off once again and Colin stepped back and watched me do it. He wasn't going to help because he wanted me to learn to be totally independent. If he kept helping me with every little thing that I needed to do that would never happen. We drove round London looking for bathroom equipment that I could use when I moved to London. Eventually, we both had enough and walked back to the car for the last time. I was more exhausted by the day than I realized and as I bent down to undo my legs for the sixth time I knew I didn't have the strength for the task. I also knew that Colin probably wouldn't help me either.

I normally needed the full width of the front two seats for my leg removal operation, so Colin had been standing outside the passenger door waiting for me to finish taking them off. I continued to struggle with the straps using my mouth and dressing stick but knew I couldn't do it. I looked up at him and said: 'Colin, you'll have to help me with these legs. I just can't get them off by myself. I'm too tired.' He could see the state I was in, so he broke his usual rule of non-interference. Leaning down into the passenger seat he started to pull off the first leg. I leaned back in the driver's seat, feeling relieved. As he got on with the job I sat up straight and looked out of the front window.

'Do you realise where we are, Colin?'

'No, I don't. Where are we?'

'Next to a bus stop.'

'Okay, so . . .?'

'You need to see this, Colin.'

What I could see was a queue of people waiting for their bus and watching us. They were all craning their necks and looking fixedly in our direction. From their point of view it must have looked as if Colin, an older man in a suit, was bending over a young girl in the front seat of a car and doing something suspicious. It looked like his face was up my skirt and it was also clear that he was grappling with my legs. I thought it was hilarious but I could tell that the people at the bus stop didn't see it that way. They looked uneasy and concerned, especially a middle-aged lady at the front of the queue. Colin looked up and when he saw the people's faces his jaw dropped. 'Come on, let's go!' I shouted. With one final jerk he pulled off both legs and went staggering backwards on to the pavement. His hair and suit were ruffled and he was gripping an artificial leg in each of his hands. I was in stitches but the middle-aged woman started screaming hysterically and we didn't stop to explain. Colin gave her a quick apologetic expression and threw my legs into the back. Then he jumped into the passenger seat, slammed the door shut, and I accelerated off into the traffic. We were laughing all the way back to Banstead.

My time at Banstead was coming to an end. I could drive

and I had my Art O-level and several sessions in the practice flat under my belt. It was time to see whether my dream of an independent life was going to be a reality or not. Colin had found a hostel in Shepherd's Bush which looked promising and we both drove up to London to check it out. It was essentially a bedsit with a communal shower and a live-in manager to help if anything went disastrously wrong. Colin was the architect and it was up to him to consult with me and assess the kind of modifications that would need to be made if I were to be able to live there.

In order for him to see how things would work for me, Colin did a very obvious and clever thing. If you want to find out what it's like being me and how I operate in the physical world, you can do the same thing that he did. He got down on his knees and held his hands behind his back as if he'd been handcuffed. Then he moved round the hostel trying to open doors with his mouth or pushing them open with his head, just as I would have to do. After half an hour or so, he had a clear picture of what would have to be changed so that I could live there.

What kind of problems was I going to face? Well, if you're disabled you have to have a key to get into your own home just like anyone else. But how was I going to use a key when I had no arms. We had to find a keypad that would work electronically and which I could access whether I was in my legs or not. It would have to be something that I could work by using my tongue or my nose, but most importantly it had to be easy, so easy that I was in no danger of falling over. Whenever that happened it was impossible for me to get up without the help of another person.

Another item I needed and which Colin went looking for was a body dryer which was essentially a kind of very big hairdryer. Colin found a body dryer and it was installed beside the shower. Next I had to try it out to see that it worked properly. I started the machine by head-butting a switch. The dryer had a letterbox slot which was moved up and down by a motor and enabled me to be dried from head to foot. When I'd finished, I was able to switch it off by head-butting it once again. It worked very well and was fun to use. I discovered that it could dry me in all kinds of interesting places. I really think every bathroom should have one.

The other problems we found were not insurmountable and we were both encouraged by the progress that was being made. Colin made the necessary arrangements for the work to be done and I prepared to say goodbye to Banstead. I had many good friends there among the staff, at the riding stables and at college, not to mention Colin himself. However, I'd never really developed an affection for Banstead as an institution and I would not be sorry to leave it behind.

I used to wonder about institutions. I could see they had to have rules to work properly but it seemed to me that often the rules were there for no good reason. I could never understand why I had to be asleep by 9.30 at Banstead. I was seventeen years old! I could see that for a lot of the staff the rules were a convenience for them and more important than the people they were designed to help. But there were always a few who were truly outstanding people. They helped me unstintingly during my early years. They never judged me by my mischievous moments and low points. They had faith in my abilities and a true sense of the real person inside my disabled body. They encouraged my dreams of independence and having a career. I just wish there had been more like them.

What did worry me was the prospect of living on my own for the first time in my life. I was now nineteen years old and on the verge of having something I had told myself was what I'd always wanted. But it scared me. And I began to look for other solutions that weren't so brutally challenging. Perhaps I could live with the family to start with and then think about the hostel as a next step after that. But Colin didn't think that was a good idea. I had talked to him long and often about my dream of living in my own home on my own terms and he didn't want me to give up when I was so close to achieving it. I took heart from his support and agreed to try the hostel, but I couldn't shake my inner fears and misgivings.

Finally, all the necessary changes had been made to the bedsit in London. After two years at Banstead they decided I was capable of living independently and my time there came to an end. It was time for me to move on.

9

Living in London

The two people who had motivated and inspired me the most at Banstead were Jenny Pearce, the senior physiotherapist, and Colin. Both had become good friends and ardent supporters of my dream to become someone who didn't have to be in an institution or halfway house, someone who could live an independent life.

They both came up with me to London on the day I left institutional life for ever. I don't know if I was more excited or more scared by the prospect of being on my own. It was what I'd always wanted but it was a complete leap into the unknown.

After we arrived and I'd unpacked my things, we sat round with cups of tea and chatted and joked. It was a wonderful moment just being with friends and with no prospect of being bossed about and ticked off for breaking some rule or other. I kept looking round at the furniture and decorations, taking it all in and finding it hard to believe I'd finally moved to a place of my own. It was only a bedsit but it was *my* bedsit. I couldn't stop smiling.

In due course, Jenny and Colin had to leave. They had their own lives to lead and work to do. I heard the front door slam and their footsteps become faint as they walked off down the road. I just sat on the bed, still looking at things: the little kitchenette designed for my height; the window on to the street; the wood chest of drawers in the corner, and suddenly all the euphoria and excitement drained right out of me. I felt empty and utterly alone. I was in London by myself in my little room and I knew nobody. It was too much and I telephoned Colin not long after he had left to ask him if he would talk to the people I had been planning to stay with to ask them if I could come to them. He was understanding and sympathetic but didn't think it would be a good idea for me to change plans. I wasn't surprised by his response. I think he knew almost better than I did how important it was for me to try to have an independent life. But when I got off the phone I felt as miserable as ever. I lay on the bed and stared at the ceiling, tears welling up in my eyes. I couldn't shake my mood. But even at that low point I knew I was going to cope with it somehow. I had to.

In fact, the hostel was a good place for me to start my independent life because there was a warden who lived on the premises and to whom I could turn if I needed assistance or advice. He was not like the wardens at the children's home and there was no question of him maintaining discipline or administering punishment. There were also other people living there, all able-bodied, who I rubbed shoulders with and got to know.

When I lived in London my life completely changed. I quickly shed the persona that I had had at Banstead. My life back there, and previously at the home, had been proscribed and hemmed in by narrow-minded attitudes and old-fashioned rules and regulations. Now I became a carefree spirit who enjoyed every day as a journey of discovery and adventure. It wasn't spectacular or remarkable to an outside eye, but for me it was as if I had been set free from prison. I made my own choices and lived my life according to my own wants and inclinations. I revelled even in everyday events such as going to the local shops and buying groceries.

Nine months later, I had moved to my own flat in Shepherd's Bush and a shop I frequented required me to cross the busy Uxbridge Road. On one occasion, I was returning from a shopping expedition laden with plastic carrier bags full of oranges and apples and other items. I still had my love for fruit. I was wearing a pair of tight jeans covered in small white stars and a skimpy, white-cotton summer top. I used to get the shop owner to hook the bags over each shoulder and I would walk back to my flat with them carefully balanced.

I was halfway across the zebra crossing when I noticed a red fire engine approaching. It was slowing because the driver had seen me. At that moment, the bag that was full of oranges split and the fruit spilled out on to the road and started rolling off in all directions. I didn't know which orange to chase and was standing there stamping my feet and effing and blinding. To their credit, four firemen immediately emerged from their fire engine and ran after my groceries. They had been laughing at my anger and my expletives but now they were coming to the rescue. They were everything a young girl expects firemen to be: handsome, hunky, cheerful and capable.

When they had collected together all my bits and pieces, they insisted on escorting me home to my flat. I asked them in for tea but, alas, they had to get back to the fire station. I don't know what they made of me, the barefoot young girl with no arms. I had many interactions with members of the public where they didn't recoil from the way I looked but behaved in a friendly and helpful manner. However, whatever attitude people chose to exhibit round me, I continued to be the outgoing, unconditional Miss London girl.

The next Christmas I was out buying a few bits of furniture for the flat. Lorraine, my social worker, was with me. There was Christmas shopping to do as well. She and I had been out at the shops and were having a cup of tea and a cake in a department store café. We were joking and messing around, like two mates, laughing about what we'd been doing, when this old chap came up to us and said:

'Watching you two has totally cheered me up. I'm really looking forward to Christmas now because you two have given me the incentive to carry on.'

We were both taken aback.

'I've just come back from major heart surgery and I've been very poorly, but I've been watching you, young lady, with all your difficulties, enjoying yourself with your friend, and you've given me a whole new lease of life.'

All we were doing was having a giggle and just being girls. So I was amazed at the way this old chap had reacted. It was the first time I'd really experienced somebody watching me and enjoying it and getting inspired by it rather than staring at me because I was disabled or funny looking. It completely turned my attitude around. I realized there could be a positive reaction to me from able-bodied people. They didn't all think, 'Oh, look, she's disabled, she can't do anything.' Since then I've had a growing realization about the positive impact I can have on people's lives. I don't do anything knowingly, I'm just living my life, but it does seem to happen.

I went a little crazy in London. I had enrolled in art courses but in the beginning they were only part time so I was able to enjoy the delights of London to the full. That meant going out clubbing and drinking with my friends. I had helped Tara to move to London and she now had a flat of her own and a job in a bank. Two male friends of mine and Tara and I made up a regular foursome and went out on the town every weekend. We were into the music of the eighties: the New Romantics; bands like the Human League and ABC; the very earliest forms of hip-hop. We were extrovert and outrageous, enjoying the consternation and the attention we got in the clubs we frequented. We would come out of a dance club and go to the late show at a cinema in Chelsea or Notting Hill Gate, emerging at three in the morning. I suppose we could be described as modern bohemians. And we bumped into all sorts of people who were part of London life.

On one occasion, Tara and I emerged from a cinema in Chelsea at midnight. We were using Tara's car, which was parked very tight to a railing. It was drizzling and I wanted to get into the passenger seat as quickly as possible. We were larking about being silly and I was shouting at Tara to get a move on with the keys and open the doors as quickly as possible so I could get in.

'Hey, Alison. Look who's behind us!'

'Never mind who's behind us – open the door!'

'LOOK who's behind us, Al!'

'What? Who? What are you talking about?'

I was really keen to get into the car out of the drizzle, but I reluctantly turned and looked behind us to see who Tara was talking about. It was Princess Diana. Her car was parked immediately behind Tara's and she was standing there laughing her head off at the two of us. She had been to her health club for an exercise session and had just come out.

'What are you two doing out at this time of night?' she asked us.

'Well, what are *you* doing out at this time of night?' we replied.

She explained that she had a very busy schedule and this was the only time that she was able to do her exercises at the health club. She was friendly and informal, and was just as radiant and charismatic as she appeared in the magazines and on television. She had no airs or graces but still emanated a regal presence and style. We stood and chatted in the rain for about twenty minutes while her bodyguard waited. She asked what we'd been to see, and what we were up to, and about ourselves. She was wearing a tracksuit so we asked her about her fitness club and which exercise machines she used and whether any of them might be suitable for us, ha ha. She had a superb Jaguar parked very close to Tara's Mini Metro, effectively blocking us in. She was driving and had to get into her car first to let us out. We warned her not to bump our beautiful car with her old banger and that we had heard about her bad driving. She laughed and said: 'MY bad driving! What about you two!!' We were three young women in our twenties having a laugh. It was as simple as that and a lovely casual way to meet her. One of those chance occurrences of London life.

We went shopping in the Kings Road Hammersmith or the Kings Road Chelsea or Covent Garden. I loved shopping and still do. When we were on one of our shopping expeditions I was always the vocal, extrovert one. I was always happy to talk to people or to respond on the few occasions that they made rude or insulting remarks. Tara would often hiss in my ear: 'What are you doing?' when I initiated these interactions with strangers. Looking back now I realize that she didn't like it, that she preferred to be more private and restrained when we went out, and that I almost always ignored her remonstrations and carried on regardless. I think she was more uncomfortable with her appearance and her body than I was and that's why she didn't like me drawing attention to ourselves by talking to people all the time.

We went to the theatre and restaurants. We did almost everything together. We both liked buying accessories and furniture for the flats that we lived in, although my taste was not as extravagant and luxurious then as it is now. I didn't have much money and I had to watch my pennies. If either us wanted to buy a major item like a sofa or a piece of carpet we would have to save for a long time before we were able to buy it. We also socialized a lot. We were making up for the years at the home when we hadn't been able to go out very much.

Until I went to the University of Brighton, most of the group that I socialized with were essentially the same crowd I had been part of at the home. We were held together by strong bonds of friendship and would meet in London, or for birthdays, or in Sussex where Dinah and Steve lived and we could visit Brighton.

Pete and Dinah and Steve, together with Tara and many others, were part of a group of disabled sportsmen and women who competed at Paralympic level. The sports group used to descend on me and stay at my flat for the weekend. We would all go out together and have a great time, and then they would continue on to their sports events in other parts of England or Europe, and, once every four years, the Paralympics. I was the one who took them to the airport and picked them up when they returned. And I was the one they left behind and I sometimes wondered whether I ought to be doing sport rather than art. But I'm about as interested in sport as I am in heaving a brick through a window, which is to say not at all. I felt quite jealous of them because they travelled to so many places to participate in their sports events and I never did. But things changed and today my travels take me everywhere.

10

Wedding Bells

I first met Francis at the Tara Hotel in London at a Mouth and Foot Painters Association conference. I was just nineteen. It was late September and I had just moved into my new flat in Shepherd's Bush. Tara and I went along together. Once again, I hadn't wanted to go to the event but Colin and Tara had persuaded me. Fran was there helping one of the disabled artists from Lancashire. Each day, after the main business of the conference was over, many of us would sit at the bar and chat and drink until the early hours. At that time I was still not a full member of the MFPA and so I didn't have to go to a lot of the meetings.

Fran was a tall, strapping lad with a fine Lancashire

accent and one night he and I got talking in the bar. He and his family were from Garstang near Preston, where he worked as a porter in a hospital. We were part of a large group, but the two of us spent most of the time flirting with each other. People say that I love to flirt and they are probably right. The atmosphere was certainly very conducive. We were all staying together in a fancy London hotel with time on our hands. And the drink was flowing – and free, courtesy of the MFPA. Fran was very at ease around my disability and seemed genuinely to like me as a person. I thought he was funny and sweet and we spent every spare moment of the five-day conference in each other's company. It was a lot of fun.

When the conference ended I returned home to my flat in Shepherd's Bush and Fran went back to Garstang. He called me the next day and on the first available weekend I went up to see him and his family. I was genuinely attracted to Fran and enjoyed being with him. I was also flattered that an able-bodied man would want me for a relationship with love and sex. That side of life had always been presented as something not really available to a 'crip' – unless they had a relationship with another 'crip'. I got the impression it was thought that no able-bodied person could possibly find me, or any 'crip', sexually attractive unless it was some kind of perverted sexual desire on their part.

I have had more than a few able-bodied boyfriends and I have never sensed that they were with me to satisfy some weird sexual desire. I think they have all liked me for who I am, for my personality and because there was a chemistry between us. But my friends who are able-bodied confirm that most people consider it weird and perverse that anyone should find me sexually attractive. It doesn't particularly bother me because I've always been able to find myself a boyfriend, but it shows yet again how far we have to go when it comes to changing the prejudices people have about the disabled.

Going up to visit Fran was an interesting experience for me. He had three sisters and five brothers who had now grown up and left home but often visited their mum and dad at weekends. So I would probably be meeting all of them as well as his parents. Word of my arrival had spread. Fran's friends and family assumed I must be a thalidomide because of the way I looked. They were also under the impression that I was rich because they had heard that all the thalidomide victims had received substantial compensation. And they had probably concluded that Fran was only going out with me because of my compensation income. As the train clattered and swayed on its long journey to the north I wondered what I was letting myself in for. But the pull of young love drew me closer to him in spite of my concerns.

Fran's parents lived in a council house in a little town where everyone knew everybody and I was nervous about meeting them. Fran had told me how when he was young his father would throw him and all his eight siblings, including the girls, out into the back garden on a Sunday night. Then they were ordered to fight each other. Anyone who didn't fight would get the belt. His father often took the belt to them anyway, particularly Fran who was the sensitive boy in the family. According to Fran, his father believed that a good punch-up in the back garden once a week would take the aggression out of the youngsters and produce harmony and peaceful coexistence.

When I arrived Fran's parents were very welcoming and totally accepted me as his girlfriend but his brothers kept well clear when I was around. They almost seem scared of my presence and when I was in the house would find all kinds of excuses for themselves to be out of it. They often tripped over themselves in their haste to get out of the door when I arrived. It always made me laugh.

Fran's mother didn't seem to have any problem and was very friendly to me. I didn't know that Fran was seen somewhat as the black sheep of the family and a bit of a loner. I think she was relieved that Fran had finally found a steady girlfriend even if she was disabled and half his height. We didn't have interests in common to chat about but she was always polite and in any case I was there to be with Fran. I had become used to the cosmopolitan sophistication of London but at weekends I would travel for three hours to find myself in a different world. I was suddenly in the bosom of a down-to-earth Lancashire family that was extremely rough and ready.

The family enjoyed the basics of life: watching football, drinking beer, renting videos and eating. They certainly were not interested in art. Although I enjoyed my weekends because I was with Fran, I soon began to hate the travelling, especially being on the train on a Sunday night and arriving in London at eight in the morning ready for my art classes. I started going up to Garstang less and less and eventually Fran decided to move down to London and stay with me in my flat. It was one of those things that seemed like a good idea at the time. When Fran moved into my one-bedroom flat I was pleased to have him with me full time. It didn't even bother me that he wasn't working and didn't seem all that keen to find a job. I had my disability allowance and the flat and we got by on that.

We were muddling along when Mike and Margie wrote to me with an offer I couldn't refuse. Nicky was eight years old by then and they thought it would be a useful experience for her if I spent a few weeks with them in their home so that she could see how I coped with my dressing sticks, how I ate and how I managed to use the toilet. They had raised the necessary funds for my airfare from the Round Table of East London in South Africa. I didn't need to be asked twice. My trip to Dallas had given me a real appetite for travel. It wasn't possible for Fran to accompany me because there were only enough funds for one ticket.

I knew nothing about South Africa but I loved the country from the first moment I arrived there. I loved being with Mike and Margie. And I loved the fact that it was completely different from England. I met Nicky's younger brother and older sister and after a few days in East London all the family and I drove down to Cape Town. I saw my first dolphins in Port Elizabeth, ostriches in Oudtshoorn and relaxed at the hot springs in Calitzdorp. The sun shone every day, the food was delicious and varied, especially the fruit, and we all enjoyed each other's company.

I don't know why we got on so well. I was a boisterous, cheeky and fun-loving young girl. Mike was a quiet man who took his work and his family very seriously. And Margie was the same – working hard and dutifully for the family's benefit. It was very traditional and a bit like the 1950s, where the husband comes back from work and the dinner is laid out and ready on the table. They were almost more English than the English. In fact, Mike and Margie found me very funny because I wasn't very English. But they were marvellous people, true friends, and I so admired and loved them for the way they had handled the situation with Nicky. They had no system of support or care as we do in the United Kingdom but they didn't abandon her. They just got on with it. She was their daughter and they were determined that she would have a normal family life. Nicky was provided with a loving family environment in which to grow up, and that was the one crucial thing my children's home didn't have.

The only thing that jarred was coming up against apartheid. I was astonished to find separate toilets for white and black people and on the occasions that I spoke to black people in the street in a friendly way, I could see that Mike and Margie were uncomfortable with my actions. I asked Margie why it wasn't okay for me to talk to black people and she told me that it just wasn't done. She didn't explain any further and I felt it would be impolite to ask any more. I realize that I was approaching the whites versus blacks situation from a very European standpoint. However, it was more than that. There were children at the home who were black, and others who were Asian, but none of us discriminated against each other on the basis of race. I had a number of black friends and I didn't regard them at all differently from my other friends. We were all the same. We were all in it together. So the situation that I found in South Africa when I first went there, the different values assigned to the colour of skin, was very difficult for me to come to terms with. However, strangely enough, I didn't feel undervalued myself.

Maybe I was cushioned by the fact that I was staying with Mike and Margie, but I felt more accepted in South Africa than I do here in England. And that feeling of being accepted remains even though there were exceptions to the rule. On one day in the middle of my holiday, Margie, Nicky and I drove to one of the many beautiful beaches along the coast to take a walk. We had got about halfway down the beach when a group of African women noticed us and began to react dramatically. They formed a rough circle around Nicky and myself and started singing in a wild ululating style. They made a number of gesticulating movements and pointed at us as if we were evil spirits and they were performing some kind of exorcism. Margie ignored them but I felt intimidated and fearful and asked if we could leave the beach. Of course, for all I know they may have been praising and admiring the two of us and our wonderfully unusual shape – but I don't think so. Every country has its dark side and, of course, South Africa is no exception. There is still a lot of superstition derived from ancient tribal beliefs. However, for me, the advantages outweighed the drawbacks. I didn't mind that the infrastructure wasn't designed for me or other people with disabilities. I was much happier in the warm climate because my body functioned better and felt stronger. It was an outdoor life which we only experience in England for a few months each year. Above all, I felt free there.

*

After a few months Fran proposed that we get married and, for some reason that is beyond me now to understand, I said yes. We had already been together for two years and I'd found him to be considerate and kind. He made me laugh, too. The fact that I was ambitious for myself and wanted to have a successful career didn't seem like too much of a stumbling block at that moment. He was the opposite of me in that respect. He was happy to have a steady, ordinary job with no particular career prospects. He liked to stay at home and drink beer and watch *The A Team* on television. He was my first boyfriend and I really thought there weren't likely to be any others.

The wedding day was a bit of a blur. I do remember how different Fran's family seemed compared with mine. My mother and Vanessa were turned out like two prize-winning models from the *Hair and Beauty* magazine annual awards whereas Fran's family was, shall we say, less glamorous. They probably thought my family were complete snobs and my family probably thought they were dirty and unkempt. I know at one point my mother took one of Fran's sisters into a bed-room to help her get made up and ready and was shocked 'at the state of her nails'.

I was completely unaware of any of it at the time. I was utterly focused on trying to get right the fundamental centre-piece of any British wedding: the bride's wedding dress. I had chosen something plain but pretty, which was in keeping with my idea that a wedding was the fairytale ending to a fairytale romance. Because of my shape and size, any dress that I wear has to be specially fitted and substantially modified. Fran and I were at a wedding fair when someone from *Brides* magazine asked if they could photograph me. I was beginning to feel very fêted and fortunate – a fairytale princess whose dream was coming true.

I admit that I felt a certain pride in relation to my mother. I was showing her that I, too, could find a man and get married, just like any other normal girl. Many of my friends, like Tara and Pete, were there and if I'm honest I was probably showing them, too.

The wedding took place at St Michael's Church in Birmingham. Fran said 'I do' and I said 'I do' and then we all went on to the Birmingham Motorcycle Museum for the reception. There was plenty to eat and drink and a white wedding cake with three tiers, which we cut in the traditional manner. Fran used his hand and I used my shoulders. Speeches were made and there was a lot of laughter. All my friends who were there said it was a great wedding and they were probably right. I don't remember much about the reception but I do remember dancing with my new husband and everyone around us smiling and enjoying themselves.

Much later Fran and I slipped away and got a taxi back to the hotel where we were staying. We took the lift to our room but when Fran had shut the door behind him, he turned to me with an odd expression on his face.

'You're mine now and you'll do as I tell you!' Fran said in his broad Lancashire accent. It took me a second to realize he wasn't joking. And that was when the relationship changed.

He didn't want me to go to college. He didn't like going out, and he didn't like me going out either, preferring that we both stay in and watch TV. He didn't like my friends and when I went out with them he became aggressive and threatening. After a few months I went to see a marriage guidance counsellor but Fran refused point blank to come with me to any of the appointments.

One night he sat me on the kitchen work surface and started to slowly pull me off by my feet. Fran is over six feet tall and as strong as an ox, and there was absolutely nothing I could do to stop him. He was laughing and saying if he pulled much further I'd fall and smash my head on the floor. I was terrified. He kept pulling me further and further, an inch at a time, but then he made the mistake of coming close to taunt me. I sank my teeth into his shoulder and hung on like a terrier. Although my teeth were clenched I managed to say, 'If you don't put me down right now I'm going to bite even harder!' So he put me down. We were both shocked and breathing hard and there was blood all over his shoulder. Fran was stunned that I'd retaliated. And furious. I was always scared of him after that and I couldn't love someone I was scared of. It made me feel too physically vulnerable. I had trusted Fran and now that trust was gone.

I went to the marriage counsellor a few more times but relations between us got worse and worse. In the end, I knew the only way to move forward would be to file for divorce. When I told him, he said there was no way he was going to leave. Every time I mentioned it he'd get blazing angry and refuse to discuss it. Finally, I got a court order to force him to move out of my flat. For months after he left, I lived in a state of high anxiety thinking he might get back at me in some violent way. However, all he did was refuse to sign any papers, so I had to wait the full two years for the divorce to go through.

11

Alison Lapper, Artist

*N*urse Shepherd says that I started playing about with paints and brushes, using my feet, when I was three. It was my favourite occupation. By the time I was sixteen I had won an art competition and there was an article about it in the local paper. Someone at the Mouth and Foot Painters Association read it and the head of the British Association, Charles Fowler, came down to see me at the home. I must have made a good impression because he invited me to become a student member and so began my long association with the MFPA. Student membership meant that I received a small amount of money each month to be used for buying paints and artist's materials. Membership was a great opportunity for me and in later years provided me with my basic income and security. It still does.

The MFPA encouraged and required us to create paintings which could be made into Christmas cards and sold. That's what provided their members with an income. At the time I was mainly painting figurative pictures: scenes from life and nature depicted in a realistic way. It was exactly the kind of painting the MFPA wanted. I was allowed to be a little stylized about it as long as I didn't stray too far from the path of realism. No blobs and splotches so wild that people might get confused about what they were looking at. A tree needed to look like a tree, a cow like a cow. I enjoyed doing that kind of painting and I still do.

I continued to see Charles two or three times a year. He was an extremely talented painter himself who was a tutor at an art college. He was also one of the very few disabled artists whose paintings sold. He was a well-spoken man of the old school; very proper in his manner but also very kind. He saw my potential and became my mentor, and through him I began to get an idea of the kind of life that might be possible for me under the umbrella of the MFPA.

My dyslexia and my year out because of the operation on my foot had left me with a lot of catching up to do academically. And that included my abilities and skills as an artist. All I had achieved so far was an O-level in art which was about as basic a standard as one could achieve.

When I came to London in 1984 I lost no time and immediately enrolled in short sandwich courses in art at Hammersmith College as well as doing A-level art there. I then did further pre-foundation and foundation art courses at the Heatherley's School of Fine Art. Charles pointed me in the right direction so that I did the courses which would give me a thorough grounding in painting. And where necessary, such as Heatherley's, the MFPA paid for me to attend the courses.

These courses opened my eyes to a whole other world. Modern Art, Conceptual Art, Fine Art – art as a combination of just about anything you cared to think of. Anything could be art. A tree didn't have to look like a tree. I was completely seduced by the possibilities. The MFPA were still my mainstay but I felt I had at last found an area of expression which was in tune with who I was.

I began to think I might be able to develop a career for myself as a fine artist and move beyond just being a disabled person who could hold a brush with her mouth and apply paints to a surface.

By the time I was twenty-five I had an A-level in art and had done just about as many courses as it was possible to do. So what could I do next? Charles thought that it would be good for me to enrol in a degree course. But where? He suggested Heatherley's but they didn't do a degree course. Someone suggested the art school at the University of Brighton. I was familiar with the town and I liked the idea of doing my degree there. There was only one problem: would they accept me?

I drove down from London and had an interview with Bill Beech, who was head of the art school, and some of the other tutors. I was very direct and upfront with the panel. I asked them to give me a chance and let me do my degree at Brighton. If after three months my work wasn't good enough they could kick me off the course. All I wanted was a chance to prove myself. I think my impassioned pleas won them over. And my status as a mature student in her mid-twenties probably suggested to them that I was likely to be more committed to my work than an 18- or 19-year-old.

Bill decided that I must be given the opportunity but when we started discussing the practical side of me joining the course the prospects didn't look good. I asked Bill if the art school building in Grand Parade had any adaptations for people with disabilities and he said no. When I asked whether they had any special housing, the answer was another no. I collected a lot of negative answers to my questions that day and it was clear that my attendance at Brighton University was going to be a groundbreaking event for all concerned. However, that didn't stop him or me.

Colin Smart stepped into the breach once again and began looking for accommodation. He found me an adapted flat in Crawley. It wasn't the best location and meant that I would have to make a forty-minute drive into Brighton every weekday. But Bill also found me a room in Falmer, which I could use if I was too tired to drive back to my flat in the evening. It had no adaptations but in those days I was flexible and fit and was able to make the best of the circumstances.

Bill was straightforward, pragmatic and positive. In those days, the art school building didn't even have a ramp for wheelchair access. In fact, there was nothing at all to assist a disabled student. We decided that I should enrol for that year and not wait until modifications were made. The idea was that I should get started on my degree course and we would deal with the problems and obstacles as we went along.

It wasn't easy. Firstly, I couldn't reach the buttons in the lifts so if I was on my own I was unable to get beyond the ground floor. Then there were the fire doors. The building had many long corridors which were intermittently divided by double sets of fire doors. The way they worked allowed me to push my way into the space between the two doors, but then I became trapped because I couldn't push my way out again. I would have to wait until someone came along with greater strength who could open the second door for me. There were many instances like that but I was as committed as Bill and his staff to being there so I shrugged and worked my way around them as best I could.

My chief support and helpmate was an indomitable and marvellous woman called Pat Elliott. She had some inconsequential work title like Administration Secretary but was, in reality, the linchpin and person who ran everything. Today there is probably a department of twenty people covering her workload but when I was there it was just Pat. She understood me and my needs and simply got on with solving things when it was necessary. I don't know what I would have done without her.

She was always up to her neck in administrative work but was ready with friendship and assistance whenever I needed them. She was the same with all the other students. Her sense of humour was deeply ironic and she made me laugh with her remarks. She was also a smoker and Bill had a no smoking policy in the art school. I would often walk into Pat's office and find her crouching under her desk with her backside in the air and her head in the wastepaper bin smoking a cigarette. The idea was that if Bill came in she could stub a cigarette out in the metal bin and pretend that she was looking for something. I would tell her there was no point because I could smell the smoke and she would spray a few squirts of perfume in the air and say: 'No, you can't!'

The fine art course was designed to allow the individual student to create their own curriculum. They could work as little as they wanted to get away with or as hard as they liked. It was all about expressing and uncovering your own vision, whatever that might happen to be.

I was given a large studio space opposite Pat's and Bill's offices. It had its own toilet and because there were no adapted toilets in the building they raised the floor in that one and it became mine. The difficulty about the toilet became a benefit to me. Normally students had to move round and change their studio space from term to term but I was able to stay where I was for my whole three years.

The art school assigned me three or four tutors who saw me for tutorials every two or three weeks. Apart from that I could choose my own artistic destiny and decide for myself what direction I wanted to take as an artist. I used to drive down from Crawley and arrive at the art school building at nine o'clock every morning. In those days, every student had to register when they came in by signing a list in the entrance lobby. It was too high for me to reach so I shouted out to Pat that I needed her help to sign the register. She laughed and said that I didn't need to. I made so much noise when I arrived that she always knew when I was in the college.

So there I was, doing a degree course in art at Brighton University and free to do anything I wanted to develop myself as an artist. What direction should I take?

In our British culture we don't like to look at our own bodies, partly because it's traditionally considered vain but mainly because our bodies, in particular our naked bodies, don't usually look that good when compared with models and celebrities, the people paraded before us every day as examples of what's considered the ideal. And the reluctance to look at our physical selves, whether with pleasure or even dispassionately, is doubly true for disabled people.

At the home, the adults who ran the institution accepted that the children there might achieve things – like my winning a painting competition. We could be intelligent, we could be competent, we might even be talented. But it was also silently agreed – and sometimes not so silently – that none of us were or could be attractive. Our lack of limbs automatically disqualified us from being physically appealing. I had adjusted to that fact during my teens after years of seeing people recoil when they realized I had no arms. I might have been a friendly, bubbly personality. I might have had a pretty face but the lack of limbs immediately made me ugly in the eyes of the able-bodied.

As a result, I disregarded the way I looked, or at least I saw myself as very far from any ideal form. It was a dead issue for me. I would never be able to play the 'am I beautiful enough' game so there was no point in thinking about it. At the same time, like so many of us, I fell under the spell of what I was exposed to in films and magazines – the bodies presented and promoted as handsome and beautiful in the extreme. And, of course, there were never any disabled bodies depicted as handsome and beautiful. How could there be? They were the wrong shape for beauty. When I later enrolled in various life drawing classes there was a much greater variety in the shape and size of bodies, but never anyone disabled. So over time I came to focus entirely on able-bodied subjects for my life painting, which I loved doing.

When I began my art degree I continued to attend life classes and produced a large number of paintings and drawings of the human form. My studio area was covered in them. I didn't think anything of it. For me, it was simply what I was interested in doing at the time. Then, about halfway through my second term, one of the art tutors, Madeleine Strindberg, was looking at all the work I'd done and said, 'I think you paint all these pictures of beautiful people because you don't want to face how you look, and who you really are.' I was stunned. It felt like a personal attack and completely unfair. I had come to university to study art, not to be psychoanalysed and criticized for my choice of subject.

After she left, I sat down and thought about it and realized it was true. I had never really looked deeply at who I was and maybe she had made me aware of something that was significant and important. Maybe.

At the time I viewed myself as a kind of happy, funny Alison. I *was* different and, obviously, I knew *how* I was different, but it wasn't something that I'd really gone into in any depth. There didn't seem any point. But her remark continued to bother me. I went off to the art library in a restless mood and began aimlessly flicking through books, using my nose and mouth to turn the pages. And then one particular book I was looking at fell open at a photograph of the Venus de Milo. It showed a white marble statue, in the ancient Greek style, of a woman with both her arms missing. There was a flash of recognition – hey, that's me! That moment was the starting point of the journey that I am still on today, looking at my own body and how I feel about myself, and how others feel about me.

I cleared away all my life drawings and embarked on a new project. I involved many of my friends, asking them to help me make modrock casts of my body. Modrock is like plaster of Paris but dries much quicker. We did it bit by bit, in segments, because if we'd done the whole of me in one go they would never have got me out. By halfway through my second year, I had a whole wall filled with plaster fragments of my body. I used to sit in my studio looking at them and thinking, 'God, you're not . . . yes, you're different, but you're not *that* different. Your torso's still made up like a torso.' My hips were a bit odd, and my legs, but on the whole it all seemed quite beautiful in its own right. It was a real revelation for me. I thought, wow, you look pretty good here, girl. And over time I became more and more comfortable with the fact that parts of my naked body were displayed all over my studio wall.

It was a wonderfully productive time for me and for the other students in my year. I was the needy one in the group and the others got used to helping me to do things. And because they helped me they also helped each other. Our level of cooperation was noted with surprise by the tutors and technicians. It was unusual. Students were known for being solitary in their work. Our group was different. We would pile into my car and go out scavenging in the skips of Brighton for material to use. Then we would bring all our newly acquired junk back to our studios and experiment with it.

Earlier when I began my degree course some of the male tutors had problems with me being there. They couldn't cope with a disabled art student and they dealt with my presence by just never speaking to me. One of them had been particularly distant and always passed me by in the corridors without a word, so I was surprised when he came into the studio one day to look at my work. He walked slowly up and down the rows of casts assessing each one. Then he stopped, turned round and looked at me: 'You've got really nice tits, haven't you,' he said.

I was flabbergasted, and confused. They were the only words he'd said to me in a year and a half. It was an outrageously sexist thing to say. But at the same time I was quite chuffed because I'd never been told before that I had nice breasts.

I worked long and hard for my final degree show and created an installation of my work which could only be reached by crawling through an entranceway designed for someone of my height. Inside I had placed selections of my bodycasts and photographs of myself in classical poses like the Venus de Milo. There were also photographs of me from the years when I was at the children's home. It must have been an intense experience for anyone who crouched their way into the room.

When I heard that the external examiners wanted to review my work I assumed that it had been too much of a statement and that they probably wanted to fail me or give me a low degree. I was astonished to find when they announced our results that I had got a First. It was a fantastic vindication of Bill's faith in me, my tutors, and all the work I had done.

12

My First House and a Surprise

I graduated from Brighton University in 1993 at the age of twenty-eight. I had put together a final year degree show and the Mouth and Foot Painters Association made me a full member. It was significant moment. It meant that for the first time in my life I had a real income and could qualify for a mortgage. If you'd asked me at sixteen whether I thought I'd ever own a house, I would have said no, how could I, but when the opportunity came I lost no time. My architect friend, Colin, who had helped me move into my first bedsit in London, magically reappeared at just the right moment and we spent a lot of time visiting properties that might be suitable. I loved it. I loved looking round houses, nosing round and checking them out. I'm sure we didn't need to look at so many. Of course, I had no idea what I was looking for.

I told the estate agents what I had to spend – around £50,000 – and asked them what they had in that price range. The house I decided on was in Southwick, along the coast from Brighton. It's been my pattern to buy rather old-fashioned houses that have been neglected and need a lot of love and care and attention. I go for houses that have a lot of potential, which was true of this one. An old couple had lived in it, and died there one by one. It had no modern appliances and no central heating. The carpets were mouldy and thread-bare, and everything smelled musty. But it had that something I was looking for, so I bought it.

The buying process was a bit of a shock. I had no idea how to buy a house and saw what looked like huge chunks of my small budget going to pay solicitor's fees and surveyors and the Land Registry. It all added up and left me with virtu-ally nothing to furnish or decorate. Luckily Colin knew where to apply for a grant so I could modify the house to make it suitable for my disabilities. But the application would take five months to come through and there would be another six months for the work to be done. In the meantime, I had nowhere else to stay, so I moved into the house just as it was. Simon, my old friend who I had previously shared a flat with, moved in with me. It was chaos from day one but the house finally took shape and we began living a bohemian life together as housemates.

Simon and I have always been on the same wavelength and share an oddball view of human existence, as well we might given our experiences at the home and in the world at large. I had my MFPA member's income, which enabled me to pay the mortgage and buy a few of life's luxuries. We were certainly able to get by comfortably. I continued to paint and Simon continued to read book after book on every subject imaginable.

We kept any hours we chose and often went for strolls in the town at 3 or 4 a.m., looking out for windows in houses which still had their lights on. We would speculate about who the people were and why they were still up and what they might be doing. Often we would fall about laughing at nothing in particular. We were a couple of English eccentrics indulging our freedom to do what we wanted.

We had Pete Hull to stay and Tara came down from London for weekends. She was keen to buy a place of her own, not too far from me, and I did the rounds of the estate agents on her behalf. When she visited we looked at some properties together and I was looking forward to having her as a neighbour and continuing our friendship and good times once again.

She had come to stay with me for the weekend in the usual way and Pete had come over from Hampshire, where he now worked in the sports department of the county council. The three of us had a great weekend together but that was the last time I ever saw her. She gave no sign of her impending change of attitude towards me. She was the Tara I had always known, my best friend. I still have the photographs that we took. We were all smiling.

I telephoned her in the week to find out if she was

coming to stay the following weekend. She picked up the phone but put it down again when she heard my voice. I phoned several times after that and got her answerphone. I was worried and concerned, and left message after message, but she never replied. We remain out of contact to this day.

What had happened? Did I say something to offend her so absolutely? Was she jealous that I had bought a house? Surely not. She was about to buy a house herself. I couldn't work it out and I've never been able to get through to her in order to hear her side of the story. I have often asked Pete about it but he refuses to say anything. I suspect that he knows the answer but has promised Tara that he won't tell. Pete is totally loyal and I won't be finding out from him.

It took a long time for it to sink in that Tara had put an end to our friendship. I missed her for months and expected and hoped that I would get a call from her in due course. And with it an explanation. I always thought that I'd been a good friend to her and her decision to cut me out of her life remains a complete mystery.

Two years later, Simon found a place of his own and I took advantage of a surge in property prices to sell my house in Southwick and moved to a bigger place in Shoreham Beach. Again, Colin Smart helped me to make the necessary modifications so that I could live there independently. He remained a good friend and supporter of my cause. Whenever he came to the south coast on business, he would take me out to lunch or dinner and, just as I had in London, I played the game of getting him to take me to the best restaurant we could find. We would share a bottle of wine and indulge our fondness for the dessert menu. Not all my friends shared my taste for the finer things in life in the way that Colin did.

I continued my painting for the MFPA and enjoyed living in my new home, which was only one block from the beach. It was a good time in my life. I still had no career as a mainstream artist but I had a comfortable income from my membership of the MFPA. I made new friends in Shoreham and kept in contact with my old friends like Pete and Simon. I was coasting along happily in my own fashion when two events took place which changed my life. The first was the offer of an exhibition of my own artwork at the Fabrica Gallery in Brighton. The space, which was a large converted church, was to be exclusively for my work. I found the challenge massively exciting. Although I didn't sell any work through the Fabrica exhibition it still marked a turning point for me. Someone at the BBC had been to the exhibition and thought I would make a good subject for the BBC1 series *Child of Our Time*.

The second big event in my life was even more significant. I had been pregnant in my twenties, had miscarried four times and had always assumed that becoming a mother was not a possibility for me. I knew the same opinion was held by all the medical staff at the children's home. But when I became pregnant again in April 1999 I knew I wasn't going to miscarry. This time I had a very positive feeling about the baby. I was very fit and healthy and everything in my body and brain felt right. It was a very active and sparkly period in my life and the pregnancy had the same quality to it.

I had been staying with my boyfriend, Tim, at his house

in the Cotswolds. I had been introduced to him by a mutual friend, Nicky, and I liked him. But I had only known him for three months so I didn't know him as well as I might. He was attentive and made me laugh, and he was very well dressed and stylish, so much so that when I first met him I thought he was gay. He was the only man I'd known who took longer to dress than I did.

Although he wasn't the love of my life I did think that we could make something long-lasting from our relationship. It wasn't just a fling and I had thought that it was more than just a fling for him, too. But perhaps it wasn't. Perhaps I was only okay for him as long as I remained light-hearted and full of fun. I had noticed that he preferred to express his fondness for me behind closed doors and had difficulties with it when we were in public. How was he going to respond when I said that I was pregnant and needed his emotional support? I was not enjoying what I imagined was the answer to that question. I had a gut feeling that he wouldn't be happy about the news. He was already a divorcé and a long-distance father to his other children.

I knew I had to tell him, so before I went to my doctor I rang him and said I thought I was pregnant. I was expecting a bad reaction but I didn't expect him to rant and rave like he did. He said he already had children and he didn't want any more. He was so aggressive and unsupportive that I got angry myself. I called him a selfish bastard and plenty of other names in the same vein. But he stuck rigidly to his point of view which was that he absolutely did not want this baby. He put so much pressure on me that I almost agreed to his demand that we terminate the pregnancy. I thought he might be right. How would I support and look after a baby on my own as a single mother?

When I put down the phone I was well on my way to the conclusion that the best thing would be to have an abortion. I decided to call my mother to see what she thought. She adored her grandchildren and perhaps she would be happy if I was going to provide an addition to that group of children who were so important to her. But when I gave her the news she was especially negative about the prospect of me having a child.

'Why'd you get pregnant? How can you look after a child? You'll never cope. You'll never manage.'

Those were some of her more polite remarks, and the rest of the family essentially agreed with her. It was a difficult time, mainly because people were so against what I was doing. And that seemed to be a common pattern in my life. The lack of support created a kind of strength in me. Whenever I chose to do something I considered a normal everyday thing, people sometimes became very opposed to me doing it. It became controversial. It became a big issue. But equally, once I decided on a course of action it was very hard to dissuade me from following it through.

Many of my friends also shook their head from side to side and looked worried when I told them, but there were exceptions. Not everyone was against the idea of me having the baby.

My friends Nicky and Sharon said to me that whenever I talked about the pregnancy my whole face lit up. They asked me why I was letting Tim dictate to me. Ultimately it was my choice, they said. I took heart from their support and began to swing back in favour of keeping the baby after all. I accepted that Tim was never going to be there for me and wasn't going to support me or the baby. However, in a strange way that realization confirmed what I had always known: I was going to have the baby and keep it. And once the decision was made I felt much better and began to find support from other quarters.

I went to my GP, Alison Smith, and she confirmed that I was pregnant. I told her about my situation and that I couldn't count on Tim or my family. She listened sympathetically and told me not to worry. If I wanted to have the baby she would support me 100 per cent. It was wonderful to hear a medical professional being so positive about my prospects. It helped my morale enormously.

I also knew a consultant gynaecologist, Mike Rymer, who had treated me some years earlier for ovarian cysts. In spite of the encouragement I had received from my doctor I was still feeling uncertain and insecure about having the baby and felt I needed the extra reassurance of his support. He was another doctor whom I trusted and whom I knew, from my previous experience with him, understood my particular needs.

I phoned his surgery to talk to him and got his receptionist on the end of the line. It had been several years since a previous conversation and she was rather snooty with me. She said that I shouldn't be calling him like this and that if I wanted an appointment I would have to arrange it through my GP. She was right. That was the proper way of going about things in the world of doctors and I didn't want to argue with her because I knew I would get nowhere. I said all right but could you just give him this message from me: 'Alison Lapper is pregnant.'

I think she was taken aback but she must have relayed the message to Mike because he rang me a couple of minutes later. He was as friendly as ever and asked me to come to see him. I made an appointment for the following week and after he'd examined me he declared that I was in great shape and looked radiant. He would do everything in his power to make sure that I got through the pregnancy safely and that the birth was successful.

I had already made up my mind to have the baby but the conversations with Mike Rymer and Alison Smith were the final nails in the coffin of Tim's wish that I have an abortion. I had already thought long and hard about the possibility that my baby would be limb deficient like myself, but Mike had told me that the chances of that happening would be as low as 5 per cent. In any case I'd come to the conclusion that if the baby was impaired in any way there was no one better in the world to understand its needs and look after it.

I had friends who had a child whose disability was the same as his father's. They had brought him up and taken care of him so well that he had an extremely positive idea about himself – and a very full and active life. It's only society and the able-bodied who have a negative view about disability and who think it should be banished from the earth. Luckily for me it was not a crime to give birth to a disabled child, but there are disturbing current trends which suggest that it might be a possibility in the future.

In the following weeks I had many discussions with both Mike and Alison about the potential difficulties of raising a child on my own, but they continued to be encouraging. Mike told me that I'd done everything else in my life except motherhood and that I might as well achieve that, too. They had a point. I had my own house and was financially stable with a job that I was very unlikely to lose.

Alison arranged a case conference with other professionals, such as occupational therapists, and social services to see whether they would be able to support me in any way, either during or after the pregnancy. Social services were particularly hard on me at that meeting. They said that I'd created the situation and would have to deal with it on my own. There was no money to help me. It was the first chapter in my chequered history with the social services department.

I continued to blossom during the pregnancy and was never ill. For the first seven months I felt fine, but then as the baby got bigger and heavier the strain on my spine turned into a nagging pain which never went away. When I was six weeks from term I went into labour. I rang my mother to ask her to come down and be with me – the baby was premature by 1½ months and I was frightened. My panic was getting the better of me and I needed her support. But she and Alan had booked a holiday and were unwilling to cancel it. I felt badly let down. From my point of view, it seemed as if their holiday was more important than the birth of my baby – their grandchild.

My neighbour, Val, took me into hospital on Christmas Eve and that was the last I saw of anyone for three days. I don't know why none of my friends came to see me during that time. I suppose they were all too involved with their Christmas activities. If they had, they would have seen how badly panicked and scared I was. I felt very upset and let down by everyone.

The hospital gave me a drug to halt the labour and I lay alone in my bed watching the baby's heartbeat on the monitor and waiting for the drug to take effect. Thankfully, the baby was doing fine and the crisis was over.

In the end it was Nicky, the friend who had introduced me to Tim, who drove down from the Cotswolds and took me home on the day after Boxing Day. By then I was emotionally and physically at a low ebb. All my strength and vibrant health of the early months had drained away and it was only Nicky's support that got me through the last days of the pregnancy. A few days later, when I had got some of my strength back, she took me to see Mike Rymer. I waddled slowly and painfully into his room feeling very dejected. He took one look at me and said: 'You've had enough, haven't you, Alison?'

I burst into tears and said: 'I can't do this any more. I've had an amazing pregnancy but I just can't cope with the pain.'

Mike said: 'Okay, Alison. Don't worry. I'll get you in for next Monday and we will do a Caesarean.'

I was so relieved. But on Monday he rang me and said that there was an emergency at the hospital and the earliest they could bring me in would be Wednesday. I couldn't believe my bad luck but I got through those two days somehow and on 5 January, Nicky and Sharon took me to the hospital in Worthing. The birth was finally going to happen. I took my television and enough clothes and accessories to last me six weeks because that's how long the hospital thought I would have to stay. It was just a guess because nobody knew how the birth was going to turn out, how quickly I would recover and what state the baby would be in. It was going to be new territory for all of us.

The nursing staff on the maternity ward showed me to my room and I lay on the bed while Nicky and Sharon unpacked my suitcases and put everything away. We laughed and cooed at the tiny little baby clothes which looked so cute laid out on the counterpane. After that there was nothing left to do and we were all at a bit of a loose end. I asked the sister if I could go out for a last meal with my friends and she said that would be fine as long as I didn't drink any alcohol. We found the best Italian restaurant in town and had a delicious meal. We laughed and joked and got ourselves into a great mood. It was a bitterly cold night but after our meal we still had so much energy and excitement in us that Nicky and Sharon put me in my wheelchair and raced me along the Worthing seafront. It was eleven o'clock at night. The wind was howling and the sea was high. Huge waves were crashing against the shore as we sped by and anyone who saw us that night must have thought we were nuts.

I finally returned to my hospital bed after midnight. I lay there thinking that was the last bit of fun I would have as a single woman without any responsibilities.

Sharon stayed in the room with me but neither of us could sleep. We were too excited. She kept turning to me and whispering.

'Alison?'

'Yes. What?'

'Are you awake?'

'Yes.'

'You know what.'

'What?'

'You're going to be a mum in the morning.'

'Go to sleep, Sharon.'

'I'm trying.'

'So am I but I can't.'

'Me neither.'

We both lay there laughing softly. I understood the words she was saying but I couldn't really comprehend what they meant. We stayed awake most of the night and were still awake when the nursing staff came in to prepare me for the Caesarean. Sharon gave me a shower and got me ready for the theatre. In the meantime, Nicky had arrived. I was very glad to have both my friends there because I was feeling increasingly nervous and apprehensive. I was going to have a needle in my neck plus another one in my back – and needles have always been my major phobia.

I was wheeled into the theatre and Mike came to see me and asked me if I was all right. Tears started to well up in my eyes because suddenly I didn't want to go through with it. Mike assured me that everything was going to be fine, that I'd done really well and we hadn't come all this way to fail now. Then he disappeared to scrub up.

His place was taken by the anaesthetist. The vein in my neck wasn't showing well so he and a nurse decided the best thing would be to tip me upside down. Then the blood would rush to my head and make the vein bulge. On the two previous occasions that he had inserted a drip needle in my neck he had done it beautifully. But I was anxious and stressed and he probably was, too. This time he needed three attempts to get it in. It was hurting me each time he tried and I started shouting and resisting. I was getting more and more stressed and my heart rate was going up. As a consequence, the baby's heart rate started to go up as well. The theatre staff who were monitoring our heartbeats began voicing their concern and so I was given oxygen. They explained that when I breathed in the oxygen it would get through to the baby in my womb and help alleviate the stress. But the idea that the baby needed oxygen because it was stressed panicked me even more. I remember Sharon, who had come with me into the theatre to be my birth mate, talking non-stop gibberish to try to take my mind off the procedures with a needle. Her distraction technique didn't work but the anaesthetist eventually got his needle into my neck and we were ready for the next procedure.

The next stage involved me being rolled over on to my side. I lay there and felt the slightest of pricks in my back. It was the needle for the epidural being inserted into my spine. The slow numbing which followed was deeply unpleasant. It started in my left big toe and slowly crept up both legs past my stomach and up to my diaphragm. I couldn't feel anything and I couldn't move anything. They pricked me with pins to see if I had any sensation left and I had none. It was as if half my body didn't exist any more. In my mind my emotions were alternating between happiness and deep anxiety.

When Mike made the cut I felt no pain but there was some sensation like a slight pulling of the skin. I couldn't see anything because I was separated by a screen from my stomach and lower torso, but I knew they were rummaging about inside my womb and I felt the 'schloop' when they pulled the baby out. At that point all I cared about was whether the baby was breathing. It was coming out early and everyone was fearful that there might be unforeseen complications. But as soon as the baby was born it started crying as it gulped its first lungfuls of air.

'It's a little boy, Alison.'

They put him on my chest and I noticed he was covered with a kind of greenish-yellow slime, which protected him in the womb. He was not pretty but I thought he was beautiful. Sharon was by my side. She kept repeating the same sentence over and over: 'This is your son, Al.'

I was crying and Sharon was crying.

As he lay on me he became quiet and I thought to myself: this is my baby. I'm sure every woman who has had a baby has experienced this and knows what I mean. It was the most amazing and overwhelming feeling I had ever experienced. I could put all the peak experiences of my life together in one big bundle but they still wouldn't match the feeling I had when they put Parys on my chest for the first time.

They cut the umbilical cord and took him off to weigh him and then Mike came back in and said that he was going to sew me up. He said it would feel like someone was doing the washing-up in my tummy and that turned out to be an accurate description.

After that they took me through to recovery where Emma Shields, the midwife, was waiting for me with Parys. He was wrapped up in a little yellow blanket and had a hat on and he was so tiny. She lay him on me and asked whether I'd like to try to feed him. I said that he'd only been born ten minutes and he wouldn't know how, surely. 'No, no,' she said. 'Don't worry about that. Feed him.' I said I didn't have any milk but she told me not worry. The milk would come through after the colostrum.

Parys was a natural. Within five minutes he was latched on and sucking away happily. I was amazed. Minutes ago I had given birth and already the baby was lying on me feeding from my breast. Unfortunately Parys was getting colder and colder because he was premature so they had to take him away from me and put him in an incubator in another part of the hospital. I felt like I'd lost him. I'd had a baby, fed him once, and now he was gone. I began to get upset but Mike came in and told me there was nothing to worry about. But for me that night turned into the longest night of my life. Sharon was in a bed next to me and I kept waking up and saying: 'Where's my baby?' I had some pictures of him which Sharon had taken with a Polaroid camera and I derived some consolation from looking at them. In the meantime, the milk was beginning to arrive in my breasts and was getting more and more uncomfortable.

By the morning I was tired out. The sensation was returning to my body after the epidural and I was in increasing pain from the stitches and from my distended breasts.

At eleven o'clock that morning they brought Parys up from the special care baby unit. Mike said Parys had had a good night and was doing fine. He didn't need to be in the incubator any more. He could stay with me. I was propped up with pillows and Parys lay on me. Those were our cuddles and hugs. And even a day-old Parys was able to find his way to my breast by himself. The nurses couldn't believe it.

I had a blissful ten days in hospital with Parys lying on me for hours on end. I was euphoric. My baby boy was healthy, he was cute, he was a blessed miracle.

13

Parys

*L*ooking after my own child was a shock. Before the baby was
born I had been a woman enjoying life on my own terms,
coming and going as I pleased. Now I was a single mother
with a baby son who depended on me for everything. And I
needed help. The Leonard Cheshire Foundation had agreed to
provide me with twenty-four-hour care for two days a week
and I had arranged for a live-in nanny for the other five days.
I couldn't do it all myself. I was breastfeeding Parys and
changing his nappies, and he was happy enough spending long
periods of time lying on me asleep. But I was tired and
drained by it. I also knew that the local social services department were watching to see how I coped with the situation.

They had made their position quite clear. If they thought Parys wasn't being looked after properly they would take him away from me and put him into care. The nanny had asked if her boyfriend could move in with her and I said yes.

It was the first time in my adult life I'd had to share my home with a stranger; in this case, two strangers. And I didn't take to the boyfriend. He walked through the house without acknowledging my presence and had only two baths in the six months they stayed. And his habit of staring fixedly at my breast when I was breastfeeding was getting more and more unpleasant. One day I came back to the house after shopping at the supermarket with Parys and found a note from her. In it she had written a long list of complaints which included the accusation that I hadn't respected her and she wasn't there to make me cups of tea. She had left me without giving any notice. They had quietly cleared out all their things over the previous week, one or two items at a time. It was day one of her five-day period of cover and I couldn't get anyone to replace her at such short notice. We were on our own.

Julie from the Leonard Cheshire Foundation was still with me and told me not to worry, but I was finding it hard not to. Social services were not funding me in any way and I was paying for help out of my own pocket. I couldn't afford a big salary and so I thought I was unlikely to find anyone, but a friend put me in touch with someone – I'll call her Molly. She seemed very nice and although she was a smoker I was desperate for someone and relieved when she said yes to my offer of a job. I felt very vulnerable at that time. Social services had made it clear that they would have no option but to take Parys away if I had no one to help me look after him.

It was hard going looking after Parys. He wasn't sleeping well at night and both Molly and I got very tired. At least she only had to look after Parys because at that time I was successfully caring for myself. Molly did well at first but after a while she began to lose interest in the job and when I criticized her for failing to do certain things she took it very personally. However, I could find no one else and had to stick with her.

Danish television took me to France for a film sequence for their documentary on my life and Molly came with us. Towards the end of our holiday there she told me that she was having a bad period and retired to her room. The next morning I knocked on her door and went in. She was lying on her bed white as a sheet and I knew instantly that this was more than a bad period. She confessed that she had had a miscarriage but refused to let me tell anyone. I didn't know what to do because Molly couldn't work at all. Fortunately, the director's daughter, Christine, was staying in the same apartment complex with her family and she took over Parys's care.

When we got back to Shoreham I had a long talk with Molly and said that we couldn't carry on. So she left.

My friends helped me with Parys and I put an advertisement in *The Lady*. The only reply came from a young man from Serbia with terrible English but I took him on because I needed someone. A fitness freak, he turned out to be the best of all the helpers that I've ever had. He got on well with Parys and knew how to handle him. My home life became very stable because Parys was being looked after well and I didn't have to worry that social services would pounce.

After five months 9/11 happened. I had no idea that it might impact on us, but it did. Our Serbian friend became convinced that the world was going to end and he wanted to be at home with his family when it happened. Nothing I could say would dissuade him so he returned to his homeland, and I was left looking for a new helper.

A friend of mine told me that his brother-in-law brought in girls from Turkey who wanted to be au pairs. He found me a 22-year-old Turkish woman who was learning English and was interested in the job. When I interviewed her she told me that she liked children and I said that I was willing to give her a try. In the beginning she was very sweet and kind to both Parys and me but as time passed the relationship deteriorated. After three months I realized that she had started hitting Parys, even though when I questioned her about it she told me that he had got the bruises from falling over. I couldn't fire her unless I caught her in the act, so for the time being there was nothing I could do.

In the meantime, she had found herself a boyfriend and began to get up for work later and later. I found out that she had given him a key to the house without telling me about it. I hated the situation we were in but I didn't know what to do about it. Finally I caught her hitting Parys and had my proof. I was angry and shocked and upset with myself that I had allowed this to happen. I hated the thought that Parys was being hit by her for all those weeks. I telephoned a friend, who came over immediately to help me pack her bags and put them out on the lawn. I couldn't bear her to be in the house for another minute.

I know it must be difficult for people who take on the job of helping Parys and me. Sometimes I'm not the easiest person to live with and my people management skills are not the best in the world, yet I still think I've been unlucky in my choices.

One helper, a Seventh Day Adventist, refused to touch me in any way after I had a boyfriend to stay overnight. Another one, a Scandinavian in her fifties, seemed mature and caring – just the kind of person we wanted. That is until the day I heard a massive thump and a crash from her room. I went upstairs on the stairlift to find her stark naked and rolling drunk on the floor. I had to call two friends to lift her back on to her bed so she could sleep it off. All in all we've had more than twenty helpers in the house during Parys's first four years and I think it has made him a little insecure. He gets to know and to trust one and then they leave. He gets upset and confused because he doesn't understand why they have to go, and then a new one arrives, another stranger, and the process begins all over again. The constant turnover of carers and the detrimental effect it has had on Parys's morale have been the most stressful part of my life since he was born, and I still haven't solved the problem.

I have always had to rely on friends to bail me out when things have gone wrong with the helpers I've employed. My two mainstays have been my friends Sue and Mary, who've helped me out time and time again since Parys was born. I met Mary through Simon. He lived in a flat in Burgess Hill and

Mary had one in the same block. Simon always kept his flat in a state of phenomenal messiness and after a while Mary couldn't stand it any longer. She would step in and blitz the place. I got to know her, too, and she soon took me under her wing just as she had Simon.

My battle with social services continued. One of the temporary helps sent them a report saying that I didn't have any control over Parys. Social services sent a professional from their department. She visited families who were in crisis and was meant to help them with their problems. On the day that she arrived I had been up all night with Parys and we were both exhausted and sleeping. It took me a while to rouse myself to answer the door, so that put us on the wrong footing from the start. Parys was very difficult that day. He refused to clean his teeth and pushed me over, and because I was tired I wasn't coping with him very well.

The woman spent four hours in the house with us, then went away and wrote a damning report. I was incensed. How could this woman have written such a report after only four hours in my home? I was summoned to social services to answer a long list of negative comments about my ability as a parent. Luckily, my health visitor, Fiona, came to the meeting. She had been visiting us regularly since Parys was born and had a much more accurate picture of what life was really like in our household. She sprang to my defence when the author of the report said what a bad mother she thought I was. There was a big slanging match between various professionals at the table and the lack of communication between different departments was very evident, but they wouldn't withdraw the report. That would remain on my file in perpetuity.

I was still incensed for days after the meeting and I decided to get in touch with an organization that helps people to fight social services injustices. In addition to the report, different people from social services had been trying to get me to claim the top rate of benefit for myself. It was intended for people who could do nothing for themselves at all. I didn't think I was entitled to it and a magistrate I knew, who helped me fill in my claim forms, told me that if I did apply for it my case was arguable. The social services department wanted me to do it because they would be able to claw back more money when I was at the higher rate. I was continually being pressurized to go along with the idea and whenever I mentioned that I thought I wasn't entitled to it they told me not to worry. It would be all right.

The organization heard my complaints and arranged for me to meet the head of social services. I explained everything to him and he was very sympathetic. He told me that I would not be harassed any longer and in due course I received a letter of apology. But the report still remained in my file. They wouldn't budge on that point.

In December 2000, I was able to return the hospitality of my South African friends when Margie and Nicky came to see me at my house in Shoreham. I had given birth to Parys eleven months earlier and had decided that I needed a bigger family car than the sporty two-door that I had at the time. The car had been adapted at great expense so that I could drive it and would be of no use to an able-bodied driver, or even a disabled driver unless they were like me. I happened to know someone who *was* like me – Nicky. I immediately wrote to the family and offered them the car because I knew it could be fantastically useful for her. The situation for a disabled person like her was much more difficult than it was for me in England. Disability is very low on the list of priorities in South Africa. So I knew the car could make a big difference.

By this time Nicky had grown up and become a serious, thoughtful adult just like her father. She was highly intelligent and I'm sure she found me very frivolous and shallow. She was doing a degree with a view to becoming a trained psychologist. She was still totally determined and always developing new ideas. I was full of admiration for her abilities, but I knew from my own experience that if she had a car it would totally transform the quality of her life and open up a whole range of new possibilities, just as it had for me. They had replied to my letter with a lot of enthusiasm balanced by their characteristic caution. They wanted to see whether it was feasible for Nicky to have a car and whether it could be further adapted to meet the requirements of her body shape. The only way they could make an assessment was by coming over to England, which they did. They met Parys for the first time and I could see how pleased Margie was for me now that I had become a mother.

The day after they arrived we all got in my car and went up to the Mobility Centre in Surrey to see what the engineers had to say. We had to find out, first, whether they could do the necessary modifications and then how much they would cost. We were all nervous. I was still being filmed by a Danish film crew for the documentary that was being made about my life. Margie and Nicky were feeling a little self-conscious and I didn't want the camera to be there. However, I had agreed to do it, so we all had to make the most of it.

After a few hours measuring and discussion, they concluded that it would be possible to convert the car so that Nicky could drive it. This was fantastic news. It wasn't the end of the story, though. When Mike got in touch with the shipping companies to see how much it would cost to transport my old car to South Africa, the lowest figure was over £10,000, more than the cost of the conversion.

Margie and Nicky returned home disappointed. It didn't look as if it was going to be feasible after all. I felt very sorry about it, too. But Mike wasn't going to let it go. In his typically determined style he kept battering away at the shipping companies until eventually one of them agreed to sponsor the car's transport to South Africa. Now it would cost them nothing for transportation and that cleared the way. The modifications were made and today Nicky drives my old Honda all over the country.

Parys is now five years old and we've been through a lot together. I am the only person who has been constantly in his life since he was born. I am his only real security. So we have a very strong bond. And even though I can't physically restrain him, he can still tell from my tone of voice when 'no' means no. I have trained him by voice to always look both ways when he crosses the road and I have heard from people that he always does it even when I'm not there. But it hasn't been easy and I wonder what effect that will have on our relationship. I have always been very open and honest with him about my disability. It hasn't ever created a barrier between us but if the children at school tease him or make negative comments about his mother he may find it very hard to deal with. It makes me nervous at times but I know we'll both get through it and come out smiling. We always have.

14

Meeting Michael

I was four and a half months pregnant when the Fabrica Gallery mounted an exhibition of my work. The gallery was a converted church in Brighton. It was a huge and interesting space for me to show my work. I had been very excited by the project and I had applied myself for months to make sure I had enough work to fill the cavernous interior. Now it was finished. I had filled the place with photographs of myself at various stages in my life – from babyhood to adulthood. I had also included recent work, which consisted of collages featuring my nude body and other elements like flowers and angel wings. I was still trying to explore and depict my own form in a way that would allow able-bodied people to come to terms with what I looked like. Of course, I expected them to experience pity and sympathy when they saw the medical photographs of me as a baby and a young child, but I also hoped that they would be able to get beyond that and see the human being in the form. I wanted them to have a sense of my journey towards self-acceptance and, perhaps, experience the first intimations of an idea that disability could be artistic and even – this was a long shot – beautiful. Some of the photographs were just of my face, shot in black-and-white in the style of glamorous pre-war film stars. Each one was set in a frame and was lying on the floor covered in large salt crystals. Beside each frame was a 3-inch-wide brush attached to the floor by a brass chain. When people first came in each photograph was completely hidden by the salt crystals and my idea was that they would kneel down and brush away the crystals to reveal the idealized portrait underneath. I thought it would be interesting to give visitors a chance to interact physically with the exhibits, instead of only requiring them to stand and look. I also hoped the softness of the photographs would counteract the hard-edged and confronting style of some of my early medical photographs.

Many people came to the exhibition and responded in a variety of ways from deep and absorbed interest to stiff discomfort and cursory glances. When I was present, a number of people used to come up to me and ask me about myself and my work. But many did not. Perhaps they were too shy. I know many able-bodied people find it difficult to approach me because they fear that they might feel awkward or say something embarrassing like 'Can I give you a hand?' The English language is full of phrases which people use every day and which contain the word hand. I have to hand it to you. The job's in hand. Hand on heart. She's a very hands-on person. And so on. It's a long list and people often use those phrases in conversation with me. A few seconds later they suddenly realize. It often embarrasses them because they think I might be offended as I don't have any hands. The truth is, I don't mind at all. I think it's funny. As long as people are not deliberately trying to be offensive, it doesn't affect me when they say things like that.

The Fabrica exhibition marked a turning point for me. Someone at the BBC had been to the exhibition and thought I would make a good subject for the BBC1 series *Child of Our Time*. I was also approached by Milton Media for Denmark's TV2 to be in an hour-long documentary about my life. That programme, *Alison's Baby*, was broadcast in many countries and won the Prix Italia and the Prix Leonardo. People seem to respond to my story and I received hundreds of e-mails from around the world. At the same time my annual appearances in Robert Winston's *Child of Our Time* brought me to the attention of the public in Britain. However, neither of these programmes focused on me as an artist.

It was a Sunday and the exhibition had already been running for a week. It was an exciting moment for me but it was also the first of many exhibitions where I didn't sell a single piece of work. I suppose what I had created was too confronting and difficult for people to contend with, although some years later one of the pieces that was shown at the Fabrica was bought by the Brighton Museum for their permanent exhibition of art. It was a collage showing me naked from the waist up, sporting a pair of white angel wings, and was edged round with a border of flowers, intense reds and purples set against the black and white of the photograph of me and the wings.

The gallery had arranged for me to be there all day so that visitors could 'talk to the artist'. I had honestly expected there to be no one who wanted to 'talk to the artist' but in a very short time there was a queue of people waiting to speak to me. I sat on some big stone steps beneath the altar of the old church and answered people's questions. For the most part they congratulated me on the exhibition and often said that they found it 'very interesting'. I was not having any really in-depth conversations and was casting my eye over the queue to look for promising newcomers. I noticed a tall man with dark hair. He could have been in his late twenties. I have always liked tall men so I looked forward to the moment when it would be his turn to talk to me. He said how interested he was in the exhibition and how moved he was by what he had seen. It had touched him in his heart. He thought I was very coura-geous to present myself to the public in such a revealing way. He didn't think he would be able to do the same. We must have appeared very engaged in our conversation with each other because the queue died away and the two of us were left talking side by side on the steps.

I am going to call the man Michael, but that isn't his real name. He had been a graphic designer but wasn't working any longer because he had mental health problems. He struck me as very intelligent and a really nice guy, so I didn't pay much attention to what he said about these problems. I knew nothing about mental health in those days, and I didn't realize that he was giving me the spiel about himself that he gave everybody. He was charming, witty and handsome. I really liked him and, if I'm honest about it, I have to say that I really fancied him, too.

But just as I was really getting to know him, he said that he had to go. I thought he was being a bit abrupt because we were getting on so well, but he gave me his phone number and I thought, oh well, I can always call him. I didn't realize that his sudden departure was part of a pattern of behaviour derived from his unbalanced mental state.

I'm an impatient person and I'm not one of those women who wait around hoping that the man will phone them. So the next day I phoned him. He was surprised but pleased that I had called and we agreed to meet at the Sea Lane café in Worthing. In those days Michael's 'thing' was to bring his portfolio with him and when I arrived at the café, after we had ordered tea, he proceeded to show me his work. I found him wonderful and enchanting to be with. He was everything I could have wanted in a man, and I had no idea that there might be a downside.

Once again, after about an hour, he suddenly announced that he had to leave because he had to go somewhere. It sounded as if he had an appointment to go to, but I discovered later that there were never any appointments and there was never anywhere that he had to go. Running away was a safety mechanism for him.

We continued to meet regularly at the café and became a

sort of couple without actually acknowledging it to each other. It was like the beginning of any relationship. We spent time together, we talked and we flirted. We talked about everything. We talked about politics and life, and we talked a lot about Michael. When I meet someone for the first time my tolerance level is very high and I have no difficulty letting them talk endlessly about themselves.

Two months after we had first met, when his parents were away for the week on holiday, he invited me home for dinner. He had prepared and cooked a delicious meal and I was continuing to be impressed by his abilities.

After the pudding we sat on the sofa and watched TV for a bit. Then he put on a videotape of a comedian he thought was hilarious but whom I found utterly boring. It was late at night. I was tired from my pregnancy, the conversation had dried up and I was thinking I really have to go home in a minute, so I was surprised when he leaned over and we started kissing. I knew from all the flirting that we had done in the weeks before that Michael fancied me but I also knew that anything new was scary for him. However, the power of sex enabled him to break through his fear. After a few minutes it became clear to both of us that we needed to continue what we were doing in the bedroom. And neither of us regretted the move we had made. We had an amazing and wonderful night together, and didn't get much sleep.

People sometimes ask me how I have sex. I usually tell them to mind their own business because I want that part of my life to be private and because I find their curiosity slightly offensive. There is an implicit assumption that I'm so substantially different from every other woman that my sexual life must be extraordinary and bizarre. Apart from my lack of arms and hands, and the formation of my legs, I am anatomically normal in every way. So I have sex the same way every woman does.

The next morning Michael got up early. I heard him getting dressed and asked him what he was doing. He said he had to go to work. His mood had changed and his voice was cold and indifferent. I was shocked. The night before he had been so passionate with me and now he could barely look me in the eye. I didn't understand it. I got dressed as quickly as I could and went home wondering what the bloody hell that was all about. The rest of the day was a miserable experience. I sat at home trying to work out in my mind what was going on with Michael, but couldn't make sense of his behaviour at all.

He rang me that night and wanted to talk to me as if nothing had happened. But I wasn't going to let him get away with that and asked him to explain why he had behaved that way in the morning.

'I was scared.'

'Scared of what?'

'Of everything. Of finding you. Of losing you. Of going crazy. Of getting depressed.'

I found it difficult to understand where he was coming from. I love life and I love living. What was I doing with this man who had the opposite point of view? However, something inside me made me pursue the relationship. We arranged to meet again and our friendship continued. Sometimes he spent the night, and we talked and made love but in the mornings he wouldn't kiss me or come anywhere near me. I hated that. At other times he would phone me up in the middle of the night, full of Dutch courage because he had been drinking at the pub. He was warm and funny when he was drunk and he often told me that he loved me. From time to time he would phone me after having had too much to drink. He would wait, sagging and incapable, on the pavement outside a pub and I would get in the car, go and pick him up and bring him back to my home. That is how it went on for quite a while.

He dumped me on a rainy afternoon that winter. He called on the phone and said we needed to talk. I could tell from his voice that he was going to end it between us. I drove to the Sea Lane café and parked outside. He had been looking out for the arrival of my car and when he saw me he came out, opened the car door and sat down in the passenger seat next to me. I asked him what it was he wanted to tell me and he recited all the usual things that people say when they're dumping someone. I listened in shock, unable to cry. Finally, he said goodbye, left my car and ran into the café.

He was leaving me just at the time when I needed him most. I was angry with him but I was prepared to let him go because my other situation was more important. I was pregnant and living alone. I needed all my strength to deal with the later stages of the pregnancy and the birth of my child.

Two months after Parys was born, I started to get phone calls from Michael once more. I always responded in a slightly hostile tone of voice but I didn't put the phone down. He would say that he missed me and that he wished that he had never broken up with me. He had only done it because he was scared.

He kept trying to justify and explain what he had done and why. His psychiatric nurse had told him that he shouldn't be going out with me. He was in too delicate a state and ought to break off relations for the sake of his health. Many of his friends had told him that I wasn't good for him because I was a disabled person and, therefore, dependent. In addition, I had just had a baby and my whole package was too heavy for him to deal with. These were horrible conversations for me because I felt so torn. I hated the fact that other people, whom I had never met, were turning him against me. It was cruel to tell me all these painful things. Through other people's opinions, he kept hammering home the message that I wasn't good enough for him.

However, I loved him. And the good times were very good and I got used to his running away. I had total faith that he would get well and we could be together on a permanent basis.

When Parys was three years old, Michael decided that he really wanted to give our relationship a go and he moved into our home in Shoreham. He was on very good form and extremely dynamic. Michael was very good with children and he established a strong bond with Parys. We even had his own son from a former relationship to stay for weekends. I would tell him that he had a great future, that he had a lovely son and that he had me.

We began to make plans. I had been given a small exhibition in Whistable and we were staying in a bed-and-breakfast on the day of the show's preview. We were lying in bed in the morning when Michael rolled over, looked me in the eyes and asked me whether I would like to get engaged to be married. I was thrilled.

However, all was not well with Michael. He'd missed out on being with his own son during his early years and that made him feel guilty and dejected.

The situation finally reached a turning point because of my foot. My bone had recently become enlarged and inflamed, and I was increasingly unable to walk with it. I went to see my doctor, who told me that I would have to have an operation, which would remove a large part of the knuckle bone to allow me mobility again. The last thing I wanted was to go into hospital for an operation again, but I had to do it. I wasn't prepared to give up the ability to walk. I knew that it would be a difficult time for Michael so I arranged for cover to take care of Parys twenty-four hours a day. Michael would be completely free from the responsibility of looking after him, but he could do so if he wanted.

The day after the operation I was lying in my hospital bed feeling very groggy and still in pain. Michael came to see me and immediately began complaining about the helpers and telling me what an awful job they had been doing with Parys. It was the last thing I wanted to hear at that moment. He was so dramatic and intense about it that it almost sounded as if they were abusing Parys in some way. I felt extremely worried and completely helpless. In the afternoon, first one of the helpers, then the other came to see me. They were both in tears as soon as they walked through the door and told the same story as Michael except that it was Michael doing the shouting and making everyone's life a misery in the house.

I didn't know what to do or think. I couldn't take any direct action because I had to be in hospital for another week. I suspected that the helpers' version of the story was the correct one, but I wanted to remain loyal to Michael.

Eventually, I was released from hospital. My foot was healing slowly but I needed twenty-four-hour care of my own in addition to the care that Parys needed. All of a sudden Michael moved out into the bedroom upstairs. I felt very unsupported by him during my stay in hospital but I had no time to think about that. My only concern was getting better and making sure that Parys was properly looked after.

Michael became more and more erratic in his behaviour. He would enter my bedroom and even if he found me sleeping he would start shouting accusations at me. Parys was being looked after; I was being taken care of, but there was no one there for him. He became so extreme with his shouting bouts that I phoned up his psychiatric nurse to ask for help and advice. However, nobody from his care network would discuss him with me. That may have been the correct policy as far as they were concerned but how was I supposed to help Michael unless I knew more about his condition and the best way to cope with it. It was the classic catch-22 and Michael continued to get worse while they did nothing.

A few days later Michael started threatening suicide. I immediately telephoned his doctor, but it took several days of repeated calls to get him to come out and see him. It didn't change anything and I received threatening and abusive rantings from him every day. The health-care worker who had been looking after me had witnessed a number of these outbursts and had reported them to the local social services department. They decided that Michael's mental condition meant that Parys and I were in serious danger if we stayed in the house. I was told that Parys and I would have to be taken out of our own home and put in a bed-and-breakfast unless Michael left. I argued with them all day, saying that I couldn't do it to him, but they insisted.

That afternoon Michael went out and the on-duty helper and I packed his two suitcases and put them outside the front door for when he returned. Three hours later I had a phone call from him. He had been picked up by the police for threatening to kill himself and they had taken him to the nearest hospital. Now he was coming back to the house. I felt so sorry for him and began to waver but, as horrific as I knew it would be for him, I wasn't prepared to move Parys and me out of our home. So I told him where his suitcases were and that I wasn't letting him back in.

He came round the next day to get the rest of his things and I tried to explain why I had made the decision to exclude him from the house. He was bitter and angry, not just with me but with everyone. I kept talking and trying to reassure him but nothing I said was getting through. After a while I stopped trying to justify myself.

It didn't end there. We continued to meet occasionally and I would still receive his midnight phone calls after one of his sessions at the pub. And for a while I surprised myself by not hanging up when he telephoned. I suppose I still had a lot of affection for him and the relationship continued on and off for a year. Finally, he dumped me for what was to be the last time. I had given it my all but something had shifted. He still occasionally sends a text to my mobile phone, usually late at night. I don't reply.

I decided to forget about the disaster with Michael and take Parys to South Africa for a break. My friend Mary, who had always been so kind, came with us. Almost as soon as he could talk Parys began calling Mary 'Granny' and she began increasingly to play that role in his life.

On this trip with Parys and Mary my love affair with South Africa deepened and I seriously began to think about relocating to Cape Town. Parys and I were having a great holiday. He was old enough at the age of four to appreciate more than just an ice cream or a trip on a cable car. So we visited hot springs and zoos and drove to the more remote and beautiful spots up-country. We did things any tourist would do. We looked at leaflets in restaurants and shopping centres and then decided to go to the places which seemed the most appealing.

For some reason I really can't understand we chose to go to the fossil park. I'd always thought of dry calcified fossils as dull and certainly not worth driving all day in the heat to look at. But I think the leaflet had a picture of a dinosaur, a very unfossilized dinosaur, on the front page, and Parys was very taken with it, so after breakfast we were on our way.

That was the day I met the next significant friend I was to make in South Africa. He was an Afrikaner called Hans Steyn and he ran the fossil park. By the time we arrived at the park, the heat had built up and I was regretting that I'd given in to Parys. It was dusty and dry. There wasn't any beautiful scenery and the fossils were laid out in the inaccessible pits where they had been found. Of course, there was no disability access of any kind. I was standing on the edge of one of the digs complaining about the state of affairs. I may even have asked to speak to the person in charge. In any case, he soon came. I looked up and saw a tall, athletic, tanned form. He had long blond hair flowing down his back and an earring. Smiling, he said hello and my disgruntled mood disappeared instantly. I looked at him more closely and noticed that Hans was completely unfazed by my disability. He asked me if anything was the matter and I said that I couldn't get into the pit because it was too far down for me to step. 'That's no problem,' he replied. In one swift move he had picked me up and deposited me next to him on a level with the fossil plain. I have always enjoyed being picked up and assisted physically by tall, strong men and I said something to that effect. Hans replied in the same vein with a wicked twinkle in his eye. I could tell that he had a great sense of humour. He started to tell me about himself and his life. Mary and Parys were strolling round looking at the outlines of dinosaurs so I was able to have Hans to myself for a while.

I was captivated. He talked about things as if they mattered. He loved South Africa and was very optimistic about the future but was also clear that it would be difficult. He looked forward to playing his own part in making the new South Africa a success story.

He also asked me about myself and how I had got my disability. He was very keen to make Africa accessible to people with disabilities and not just able-bodied tourists, and we talked about that, too.

I had not expected fossils to be interesting because I generally prefer things that are alive to things that are dead. But Hans made them fascinating and I enjoyed his conversation and his company. The next two hours seemed to go by in two minutes and it was time for the park to close. Once again he effortlessly lifted me from the pit, put me and my wheelchair in his pick-up and took me to my car. I was sorry to say goodbye. He had been fun to be with but I assumed I would not be seeing him again.

As I was leaving I asked him if he knew of any beaches nearby where we might be able to catch sight of dolphins. I had always been fascinated by these creatures since seeing them on my earlier visit and I had read in the guidebooks that they frequented this particular stretch of the western Cape coastline. He wrote down a set of directions on a piece of paper. He explained that I would need to be there early in the morning, no later than six o'clock, and that I might not necessarily see any. It was a privilege to see dolphins swimming and they didn't appear for everyone. He knew people who had been on dolphin watch for ten days and not seen a single one. He ended by saying that if I had any difficulties I should give him a call. He had written down his phone number. I thanked him for all his help that day and we drove off with Parys waving madly out of the back window. That night we slept at a hotel not far from the place where Hans had said we might see dolphins.

The next morning at six, we all drove to the beach Hans

had described and stood on the shore. We were bleary-eyed but about a quarter of a mile out at sea, in the early morning light, we could see the characteristic undulating movements of dolphins on the surface of the water. We stood there pointing and marvelling and feeling a little smug about our early start and sighting dolphins offshore.

I was so proud of our success I decided to ring Hans and tell him that we didn't need his help because we had found some dolphins. Hans picked up the phone and immediately knew who I was. He asked me which beach I was on and then said he would come and join us and watch them, too. He was a very spontaneous person and a true nature lover.

Twenty minutes later his pick-up drove up the road and parked next to my hire car. He bounded towards us with a big smile on his face and said 'So where are these dolphins of yours?'

I felt so proud and gleeful. There I was, the disabled English tourist, showing the experienced South African safari man where the dolphins were.

'Over there, look. Can't you see them?'

Hans started laughing.

'What's so funny, Hans?'

'Alison, those aren't dolphins.'

'Really? What are they then? Whales?'

'Alison, they aren't whales and they aren't dolphins. What you've been looking at for the last hour is kelp.'

'Kelp! What do you mean kelp?'

I looked at him to see if he was being serious. I guessed that he loved to play the joker with innocents like myself who didn't know the country. I had another look at the ocean and, of course, it *was* kelp. It was a bit brighter now and I could see the heavy ropes of seaweed floating on the surface and moving with the rhythm of the waves. We all laughed. Hans said: 'Never mind your dolphins, Alison. You can see them another day. Why don't you come to my place for some breakfast?' I said it was too early and we couldn't disturb his family at such an early hour. I was being very English but Hans insisted. He jumped into his pick-up and clattered off down the coast road. We followed him and wondered where we could be going because there was no sign of habitation, just the coast for mile after mile. And then, in the middle of nowhere, we saw his house, all by itself, right on the beach.

It had been a fish smokehouse a long time ago. Hans and his wife, Mariki, had bought it and converted it. They loved the unspoilt beauty of its remote location. I watched Hans drive up to the front of his house and then he seemed to drive straight into it and disappear. In fact, he had driven into the garage, which had no separating wall between it and the main sitting room. I had never seen anything like it. It was the ultimate open plan arrangement, a house where dogs, people and cars all shared the same space. At the far end was a set of big glass doors which ran the full width of the room. When you opened the glass doors you stepped out on to the beach and found your-self looking straight at the ocean. It was breathtaking.

Hans introduced his wife, who welcomed us to their home. They had guests staying but it didn't seem to matter. They were both so open and hospitable and friendly. Mariki swept me up in her kindness and love. She was very subtle. I

could see that she was aware of my needs and whenever I
needed it she was there to help me, but in a very unintrusive
way. From the very first they treated me like a friend.

They made us a delicious breakfast and then took us out
through the glass doors on to the beach. Almost on cue we saw
dolphins swimming and diving just offshore. Hans couldn't
resist a little tease.

'There, Alison. That's what dolphins really look like.
Kelp is very different, more green in colour, and it never
jumps out of the water.'

These days I find it hard to differentiate between my love
of South Africa and my love of the friends I've made there. In
spite of all its problems I am still drawn to the place. I have
been on holiday to many destinations in Europe but South
Africa is the only place where I return to England not feeling
disappointed with my trip.

15

The Statue in Trafalgar Square

*I*t was January 1999 when I received a phone call from an artist called Marc Quinn. I had been expecting him to ring me because Pete Hull had been modelling for a series of statues which Marc had been creating – all of disabled people – and he'd suggested that I'd be a good subject. What kind of weirdo would want to do sculptures of disabled people? I was extremely suspicious. I thought he might be just another one in the long line of people who have exploited disability and used it for its curiosity value. However, when we talked I realized Marc wasn't interested in disability in the way that most people wanted to depict it. He wasn't pitying or moralizing about it. After we spoke for a while, I knew it wasn't a freak show or some kind of weird sexual focus that he was aiming at.

He said that old sculptures where the limbs have already fallen off through the wear and tear of time, have come to receive an unconditional acceptance of their beauty. With those pieces of work providing a certain context from art history, he wanted to make equally beautiful sculptures of people who had been born naturally without limbs. He wanted to explore the relationship between the notion that we are called disabled, imperfect bodies, and yet these ancient statues are considered to be the height of beauty. Why? What's the difference? Nobody had sought to recreate new arms for the Venus de Milo and cement them on. The statue was considered perfect just as it was. He said that when disability is documented in art or science it's always presented as a kind of show of extreme imperfection, somehow always shown as grotesque or ugly. He wanted to do something different – to create something that was beautiful, something that would show that the disabled form is beautiful.

I had already been exploring this for many years in my own work. So I didn't feel that he was doing the statues for the wrong reasons. In short, he convinced me. Marc was very enthusiastic and keen to meet but I was feeling desperately ill at the time. I said I was sorry but I couldn't do any sitting for him. And that was that. There would be no Marc Quinn statue of Alison Lapper.

I was desperately sorry to turn him down. My friend Pete told me how much he had enjoyed working with Marc. I also knew that Marc was one of the foremost British artists of modern times and it would have been a tremendously inter-esting experience to collaborate with him in the making of the statue.

Many months went by and, out of the blue, Marc phoned me again. He asked how I was and whether I would be inter-ested in modelling for a statue. He was still keen to do it if I was. I gave a half-chuckle and told him there was no point in sculpting me now since I was nearly seven months pregnant. His reply surprised me and is typical of his open-minded and fresh attitude. 'That's even better!' he said.

I paused. This is crazy, I thought. I wasn't at all sure about doing it. I was feeling very heavy and the baby inside me was putting a great strain on my back. It was almost impossible for me to walk any more without toppling over. But his enthusiasm and openness to the fact that I was preg-nant were persuasive.

I thought about it a lot after his phone call. I was both excited and nervous. In most societies, even in Britain today, pregnant women are not considered to have a beautiful shape. On top of that short little people, who are missing both arms, are generally considered even less beautiful. I was someone who currently combined both disadvantages. How could Marc possibly think I was a suitable subject for a sculpture that people would want to look at? Statues are created and exhib-ited to give pleasure, to be admired. Would anybody be able to admire the statue of a naked, pregnant, disabled woman?

A few days later Marc rang me again to see if I was still keen to model for him and we talked some more about his approach and the ideas behind the creation of the statue. I saw that Marc was a kindred spirit. I had been working with my own naked body for many years as part of my creative output. He had also used his naked body as part of his work.

Of course, it did strike me that the statue was exactly the sort of thing that I should have been doing as a continuation of my work. I was also well aware that at that stage in my career I would not be able to buy a huge block of white marble and bring together the resources to make a statue of my own. So I had mixed feelings, but ultimately it struck me as a rare opportunity. I might never get pregnant again. I also knew that if I did manage to make a statue of my own it would probably never get to the major galleries or receive the kind of exposure that Marc's statue would.

I was very open with Marc about my thoughts and feelings and he was very understanding. He discussed my views as an artist, not just as the model. I both liked him and trusted him. In the final analysis I found I had an overwhelming desire to model for the statue. I knew the process of making the cast would be long and arduous for both of us, but I had experienced it before at university when I had made casts of myself for my art exhibition. And the constant visits to the workshops at the children's home to be measured for this or that had made me very familiar with this type of procedure. So I agreed to model for the statue that Marc wanted to make.

It was a cold winter's day in late November. Marc sent a car down to Shoreham for me and I was driven up to London. He realized that as I was in the late stages of pregnancy I would be tired and hungry when I arrived. He was great about it. He made sure I was fed and we chatted about what was

237

going to happen. He didn't rush me at all and there was a very friendly atmosphere. The BBC were there filming me for BBC1's *Child of Our Time* series and that was an added pressure but Marc kept everything on an even keel. He was kind and calm and led me into it very gently.

The studio was like a big white box and in it were me, my PA, Marc, his chief assistant, Noel, two other assistants and the two-person BBC film crew. When the time came for me to take my clothes off I did get a little bit nervous. I don't know why because I'm very used to being naked.

Off to one side there was a little changing room with a shower. I took off my clothes in there and came out into the bright light of the white square room. I was wearing a small robe which Marc slipped off my shoulders. I wasn't completely naked. I had on an old pair of knickers because I knew when the time came for the plaster to be pulled off they would be shredded and destroyed in that process. I was still feeling nervous as Marc lifted me on to the hard flat table. It had to be hard so that my contours would be clear. I would have loved to sit on a nice comfortable sofa but there couldn't be any cushioning of my body if the casting process was to work properly.

First, they covered every square inch of my body with Vaseline, which made me feel very cold. The Vaseline had to be spread on with great care because if they missed any part of my skin it would really hurt when they pulled the cast off. By this time, I had got over my embarrassment of being naked in front of two men whom I didn't know. Marc just kept chatting to me the whole while in the same way that he would if I had been fully clothed and that helped a lot. He had certain ideas about what he wanted. He was sure he wanted me to be seated, not standing. But he still involved me in a discussion about what would be the best pose to take – what was the most comfortable; what was the most uncomfortable; which had the best lines and contours. It felt more like a collaboration than anything else.

After the Vaseline they smeared on the wet plaster bandage, layer by layer. They did the front part of my torso first, then my legs, my back and, finally, my neck and head. The whole process took many hours and for most of the process I could only drink liquids. Towards the end I was getting very tired.

Marc and his helpers were fanatically meticulous about the casting. For example, they would plaster the front of my leg and create a section of cast from that. Then they would do the back of my leg so that they would end up with two pieces that would be joined together to create a three-dimensional shape. The front casting would have a little bit of overlap, and so would the cast from the back. Very careful measurements were made to ensure that when they eventually cast the whole body they were actually casting me as I really was and not me plus bits of overlap. By the end, hundreds of measurements and photographs were taken to make sure that the final result was as perfect as possible.

At one point they ran into difficulties trying to work out the best approach for the casting of my legs. I remembered some of the techniques which had been used in the workshops at the children's home to create the artificial legs that I walked with in those days. I explained some of the engineering tricks to Marc and he then adapted those methods so we could carry on with the work.

I was very apprehensive when they came to the part where they covered my face, first with Vaseline and then with strips of wet plaster. It was like being encased in a kind of white hell that I was never going to get out of again. I could still hear what was going on and I could breathe, but I couldn't see anything at all and I couldn't speak. My mouth is like a limb for me. I paint and write with it. If I can't use it I have no other way of letting people know what I want or need. However, Marc was reassuring. He kept telling me that it would be okay, that it wouldn't take very long and that if I got into any real difficulties just to wriggle a lot and they'd pull all of the plaster off me instantly. When they started applying the strips I got the giggles and they had to stop while I composed myself. The wet plaster was initially very cold but then as it dried it very quickly became warm and then hot, very hot. It was like being in an oven. All through the day I experienced alternating extremes of hot and cold.

They put the layers on one by one, ending up by covering my eyes. The only uncovered surface was two holes next to my nostrils so that I could breathe. I sat very still in the claustrophobic darkness waiting for the plaster to dry. There are two things I remember about that day: the interminable minutes of staying perfectly still while the plaster dried and the muscles in my back being less and less able to support me in an upright position. As the day wore on, Marc had to kneel behind me and physically support my weight because I was no longer able to do it on my own. Eventually, I was leaning more and more of my weight on Marc and he had to work harder and harder to keep me in my original position.

It seemed to take for ever and there was no point in them asking me if I was okay because I couldn't nod my head. I had to be still. Eventually the plaster dried and they pulled it off. All my make up – my lipstick, eyeliner, eyeshadow and foundation – had all been absorbed by the Vaseline and transferred itself to the inside of the plaster mask. It was strange to look down and see my inverted made-up face looking back at me from the cast.

In spite of the Vaseline the plaster still managed to stick to my skin, probably because of all the fine body hairs. When they cast my lower torso and hips they found that the dried plaster was sticking to my knickers like it had been glued, as I had predicted. They had to very carefully prise off the plaster so that the cast wasn't damaged. In the process, my knickers had to be cut to bits with scissors.

Except for the part where my face was covered in plaster, Marc and I talked about many things during the day including my progress as an artist and the effect that my pregnancy had had on my work. We also talked about the fact that I was still very much on the fringes of the professional art world. I told him that I still felt like I was on the outside looking in. He described how he had worked slowly and steadily towards establishing himself. It was all about producing the work and proving yourself by the quality of your creation. As he became better known, he was able to work in a bigger studio and use more expensive materials to create more complex and unusual works of art. I told him that I didn't like all of his art and that

I didn't understand some of it. He didn't seem to mind. I grew to like him more and more as the day went on because he behaved and worked in a very direct and down-to-earth manner. I felt he was right there with me in all the wet and mess, always as hands-on as possible and not at all detached or remote or aloof like some artists when they are creating.

Finally, Marc lifted me off the table, joking about how heavy I was because I was carrying a baby as well. By this time I was quite a sight. Every time they took a newly cast, dry piece off my body they left behind many little bits of plaster, which were still stuck to me. By the end of the day I was covered in these little bits of residue, which were extremely itchy. I was exhausted by then and the warm shower which rinsed off all the bits of plaster was heaven, and so was being dried in a big fluffy towel by my helper. I flopped into the back of a car and was driven back to Shoreham late at night.

Several months passed and eventually the statue was completed in its final form. When Parys was five months old, Marc asked us to sit for another statue. My boobs were huge from breastfeeding Parys and my stomach had slimmed down, so I was happy to have that version of me made into a statue. I was also very flattered that he wanted to make a second statue of me. Of course, we couldn't cover a 5-month-old baby in plaster so Marc put him down on a bed and took hundreds of photographs and measurements and his statue was made that way.

Months later, he invited me to the opening of his exhibition at the Cube2 Gallery in London. It was a glittering event, with an endless flow of stylishly clad arts people streaming in and out. I was also being filmed by Japanese television this time. The statue of Parys and me was attracting a lot of attention from the guests. The smooth white marble and the way Marc had taken my form and created a work that seemed perfect took my breath away. I loved it. Of course, lots of people came up to me in the gallery and asked how I was and praised the work and wished me well. I enjoyed the attention but it was Marc's statue, his conception and execution. I was only the model.

After looking at the statues for a while I realized something. The marble had no life in it, no personality. I was very excited and happy to be there but I felt divorced from the statues themselves. The statues seemed to me more like death masks. It's what I imagined I would look like if I was dead. So it was like walking round a quiet, dead Alison Lapper. Not like me at all. The one thing I still loved about the statues, though, was that they sparkled. The white gleaming marble had that quality to it and in that respect, because I love sparkly things, it reflected me very well.

I had no particular thoughts at the time about the sculptures' future. I had no idea where they would end up after the exhibition. It was an idea that Marc had been playing with and brought to a beautiful fruition, but I don't think even he knew what would happen to them next. I hoped that whatever the future of the statues my association with Marc would continue.

I always felt that he was genuinely interested in me and my art and maybe he would be able to help me in my career. But I didn't know in what shape or form. Maybe it would be something as basic as meeting people from the art world at his private viewings. I had no idea what Marc's view of me was, but I did notice that whenever the sculptures came up in conversation, or when he was being interviewed, Marc always said who I was and what I did. He never tried to keep me anonymous. Even so, I understood that I was essentially the model for a piece of work that Marc had created. And that was all. At the time of that first exhibition I didn't have the slightest idea that there was going to be a much bigger relationship between the real-life Alison and the statue which Marc had created.

I returned to Shoreham and carried on with my own work as an artist. I also faced the daily challenge of looking after Parys.

Four years went by. I received a phone call from Marc and he told me that he'd entered the sculpture, *Alison Lapper Pregnant*, in a competition and if it won they would make a much larger version which would be displayed in Trafalgar Square. I wished him good luck and didn't think much more about it. It seemed very unlikely that they'd choose a statue of a naked, pregnant, disabled woman to be put next to the likes of Lord Nelson, King George IV and the other great men of history who already had statues there. I left for a holiday with my friends in South Africa and, relaxing in the sunshine on the sandy beaches of Cape Town, forgot all about it.

Four weeks later, I was on the beach sipping an ice-cold drink and feeling quite satisfied with my tan when Marc phoned me on my mobile. *Alison Lapper Pregnant* had been chosen for the Fourth Plinth! I was excited and pleased, but I had no idea it was going to cause such huge controversy. Most early comments were critical and disparaging. It was bad art. It was too politically correct. There were others more deserving. Someone said it had been chosen by a small clique of conceptual art enthusiasts and would have no appeal for anyone else. Then after a while my story, the story of the person who was the model, began to appear in the papers. The general opinion began to swing the other way. Some critics became less critical and others began to praise the concept and write articles describing me as a brave single mother overcoming the difficulties of being disabled.

I appeared on all the television channels and was asked the usual questions. How does it feel to have been chosen over the Queen Mother? How does it feel to know half the world is going to see you naked? To the first I said it would have been a very safe old-fashioned choice, but we are in the twenty-first century after all. And the nakedness? Well, nakedness doesn't bother me now. I have artworks of mine that show me naked all over my house. My son sees them. Everyone does. I think most of the people who object to the statue do so because it's brought up their prejudices – the fact that they're not comfortable with nudity, pregnancy and disability. Maybe, over time, as they get accustomed to it, the statue will help people become more comfortable with their own bodies because, I can tell you, it's a great feeling.

When the two sculptures that Marc did of me were at the Liverpool Tate, they asked me to go up and talk about them, which I did. I also had an opportunity to talk about my own work. The audience largely consisted of disabled people and I welcomed them, but I still yearned to talk to a broader range of people than that. Once again, it made me question the whole concept of the debate in society about disability. I have the impression that the able-bodied majority just can't be bothered with it. They aren't interested in exploring the issues or seeing the aesthetic beauty that may lie in the depiction of impaired forms. If we walk along the beach and find a stone with a hole in it, we don't look at it with revulsion simply because most other stones don't have holes in them. In fact, we may be entranced by the variety of shape that the stone with the hole has brought to our attention. However, we don't respond in that way to the human form when it varies too much from the accepted norm.

I have been accused of being a terrible artist and that's why I don't sell, but I cannot bring myself to believe that. It just doesn't seem true to me. At this point in history I think my subject matter is too confronting and disturbing. People don't know where to place it in their mind, they don't see where it fits into the scheme of things. And that's why I haven't been successful as an artist so far. Somebody once said to me: 'Alison, nobody wants to put a picture of a disabled person on their wall at home.' I could see some truth in that but I think one of the purposes of art is to help people change the way they see things. I believe that the work I do will help people to see disability in a new and positive light. I have talked to Marc about it several times and all he has ever said is that I should keep going, keep producing work. And that's what I shall do. I have no intention of ever giving up my work as an artist.

At the moment there is a fierce debate going on in my

mind as to whether I should continue creating pieces that deal with disability as an issue or whether I should find a new direction for my work. I haven't resolved it. How can I take back myself for myself now that the statue has become Marc's signature piece? But certainly one of the questions that crosses my mind is this: how can I ever surpass the statue that Marc has made of me and which is going to stand in Trafalgar Square? In many ways I think it makes the ultimate statement about disability: that it can be as beautiful and as valid a form of being as any other.

Of course, the statue has had a big impact on my life. My work as an artist has come to the attention of a much wider public. I was very quickly offered an exhibition at a major West End gallery and I was asked to become one of the Eyestorm Britart group of artists. I have been interviewed by journalists from all over the world, not just asking about my life as a disabled single mother but about my work, too. It is too early to say what the effect having a sixteen-foot high statue of me in Trafalgar Square is going to be. I think it will have a big effect on people all over the world, whether they see it on the plinth for themselves or in a magazine or newspaper article. I think they'll be quite curious about Ms Alison Lapper and want to know more about who I am and what I'm like. And I think I'll enjoy the attention – I usually do.